mini style GUIDE

25.5mm

mini style GUIDE

An Introduction to Good Writing and Manuscript Presentation

Denise O'Hagan

First published 2018 by
Black Quill Press, Sydney

Reprinted 2019

info@blackquillpress.com

ISBN 978-0-6480020-5-5 (print book)
ISBN 978-0-6480020-4-8 (e-book)

Edited by Mario Baghos
Index advice Fiona Sim
Design input Embellish Creative

A catalogue record for this book is available from the National Library of Australia

FOREWORD

'Be a good editor. The Universe needs more good editors, God knows.'

Kurt Vonnegut, Letters (2012)

With the ubiquitous spread of the Internet, personal computers and digital devices, and DIY websites, blogs and e-books, the barriers to publishing for aspiring authors and writers are lower today than at any time since the invention of the Gutenberg printing press.

But the barrier between writing and good writing remains high. And it surely explains why so many writers first and foremost thank their editors in forewords, dedications and acknowledgements!

Not all writers have the luxury of editors. Whether you are an aspiring or published author, writing technical reports or project proposals, drafting a CV or job application, or even blogging, without an editor, like me, you will likely rely upon weighty reference tomes, google searches and online grammar apps for editorial guidelines.

Having searched in vain for a simple reference to recommend to writers, Denise O'Hagan 'gathered together her notes' from years of working as an editor in the publishing industry and at Black Quill Press to produce this *Mini Style Guide*. And it is a well organised and accessible resource for all writers.

With real-life examples, the guide explains clearly the concepts of good writing, including styles, misused words, variant spelling, British and American English, tricky singulars and plurals, the perils of possession (not forgetting the perennial *it's* v. *its*), and the benefits of using Plain English and the rules for doing so.

The guide then looks at manuscript presentation. This section is of relevance whether your 'manuscript' is a fiction or nonfiction piece, a report or proposal, or any other form of writing. Formatting, pagination, headings, quotations, bibliographies and references, and the correct use of citations are as important to the writer of an essay as they are to the author of a book.

Finally, the guide explores publishing options, traditional versus independent and self-publishing, and provides an extensive author's checklist. There is also an appendix, with standard forms, letters, and style templates, a glossary of common terms used in printing and publishing, and a helpful reference section of recommended resources for writers.

Denise O'Hagan has produced a guide that can be read and enjoyed in its entirety (note the possessive *its* without an apostrophe!) or simply for reference purposes. In short, with the *Mini Style Guide* on your desk, you can be a good writer and a good editor!

Robert Fairhead, editor and writer at TallAndTrue.com
Sydney, 2018

CONTENTS

PREFACE

The publishing industry can be daunting to the newcomer and notoriously difficult to penetrate. This guide seeks to dispel the confusion surrounding an industry which ultimately depends on an influx of new and aspiring writers, and inspire you to put pen to paper—or finger to key—and get started!

This book grew out of questions put to me by friends and colleagues while I was editing their manuscripts. Whether they were writing for professional purposes (as in dissertations or business documents) or for personal reasons (as in fiction or personal histories), a clear pattern began to emerge in what writers found confusing.

I looked for a simple guide to recommend, but couldn't find one. Wonderful resource though the Internet is, the sheer volume of information on offer requires a certain knowledge to evaluate. Book publishing companies have their own in-house style guides, but they tend to be brief, concerned with the finer points of house style and available exclusively to contracted authors and copy editors. At the other end of the spectrum, established style manuals such as the *Oxford Style Manual* (UK) or the *Chicago Manual of Style* (US) are highly detailed and comprehensive, but unsuited to a writer grappling with the intricacies of the English language and manuscript presentation who may be wondering, after having finally finished writing, 'what next?'

So, gathering together my own notes, I decided to write a guide myself, keeping explanations succinct and liberally sprinkled with 'real' examples. I refer to it regularly, and equally regularly continue to draw on it to help others. In making it universally available, my hope is that it may inform and encourage writers of all material by offering a clear, accessible introduction to some of the trickeries of the English language; stylistic tips on how to present your manuscript; and a brief rundown of publishing options. This last was written in response to the increasing desire to 'be published' and the surge of self-published books.

Despite all the rules governing the way we speak and write, language is elastic and constantly being stretched in new and exciting ways. I'd welcome constructive feedback and suggestions for improvements. Please send your thoughts to info@blackquillpress.com.

Thank you and happy writing!

PART ONE:
Good Writing

Styles of writing

If any man wishes to write in a clear style, let him be first clear in his thoughts …

Johann Wolfgang von Goethe, German writer, 1749–1832, quoted in Conversations of Goethe, *Kessinger Publishing, Montana, 2005, p. 79*

What you are saying, and to whom you are saying it, determines *how* you say it. As a writer you share a special relationship with your reader, so consider the nature of your address and the level at which to pitch it.

Writing can be divided into two main categories: factual and non-factual. We encounter factual writing in newspapers, business letters and the like, and more so if we read histories and biographies. When we seek out fiction, poetry and drama, however, we do so largely for pleasure, drawn in by the power of imaginative writing.

Factual writing

The aim of factual writing is practical: to convey information. Both the depth of subject and the level of linguistic complexity are determined by the readership. If you're targeting professionals, you may assume greater knowledge of the subject and familiarity with terminology, and your language will accordingly be more sophisticated. On the other hand, if you're addressing the general public, you will use short, direct sentences, explain technical or specialised terms in simple, informal language, and use visual displays where possible.

Compare, for example, these two extracts:

> The beauty industry is opaque and many harmful chemicals are silently present in everyday products. Product labels should be scrutinised, and the alternative and compound names of listed chemicals examined.
>
> To cite some examples: parabens (methyl, ethyl, propyl and butyl) are also known as hydroxy methyl benzoates; the toxic chemicals phthaltes are used as solvents and plasticisers in perfume, shampoo and nail polishes; formaldehyde precursors such as quaternium-15 and bronopol are widely used as preservatives in baby products (though not carcinogenic themselves, they can break down to release harmful formaldehyde).
>
> Increasing awareness of such chemicals has boosted the organic beauty business as it has the organic food industry.
>
> Health industry specialist's notes

> Read product labels carefully. Some chemicals go under different names. Here are the main chemicals to avoid, their various names, and where you might find them:
>
> - *Parabens* (methyl, ethyl, propyl and butyl), also called 'hydroxy methyl benzoates'—beauty products.
> - *Phthaltes*—perfume, shampoo and nail polishes.
> - *Quaternium-15* and *bronopol*—baby products.
>
> Paraphrased version of the above

The same information appears in both extracts, but whereas the first is directed at people within the industry and assumes an awareness of both the products and their marketing strategies, the second is a simplified summary for a general audience that avoids the subtler distinctions. This difference is reflected in the typographical design of the respective extracts. The first relies on straight text and paragraphing; the second uses a bullet list and italics to help the reader quickly grasp what the main chemicals are and where to look for them.

Not all factual writing is transparent. Any category is by definition limited, and some writing that is primarily informative (such as that in travel books or journalism) is memorable because it takes elements from other types of writing and weaves them together to create something new.

Consider these two descriptions of Cairo at the turn of the century, for instance:

> Occupied Cairo was a city of veils and mirrors. Britain exercised power from behind a screen of niceties, downplaying its role as first among equals of the controlling powers. The khedive stayed on his throne and sustained his nominal allegiance to the Ottomans. Britain's consul–general merely 'advised' him as to who his ministers and what their policies should be. Like the khedive himself, these morning-coated, tarboosh-capped officials were shadow puppets: European under-secretaries made sure they jigged to London's tune.
>
> M Rodenbeck, *Cairo: The City Victorious*, Picador, London, 1998, pp. 173–4

> By 1900 Britain's control of Cairo was strong though less evident. The khedive kept his throne, paying formal allegiance to the Ottomans. In theory he was simply 'advised' by the British consul–general on who his ministers should be and what policies they should follow, but in reality he remained an instrument of European power.
>
> Paraphrased version of the above

The passages are equally informative about Cairo under British rule and the relationship of the British consul-general with the khedive and his ministers. The first passage, however, expresses itself with eloquence and lyricism, giving us the flavour of the times: against the backdrop of Cairo as a 'city of veils and mirrors' which hints at layers of secrecy and self-deception, the khedive's ministers dance like 'shadow puppets' to the tune of their colonial masters, a playful image which evokes the real power behind the scenes.

By contrast, the second passage simply extracts the unadorned facts in a straightforward manner, devoid of emotion. Directed at younger readers, it aims to elucidate rather than delight.

Non-factual writing

If the boundaries of factual writing are nebulous, those defining non-factual or imaginative writing are more so. In 'creative writing', the hallmark of fiction, styles of expression vary. All, however, draw us into a created world and keep us in a state of suspense: we not only want to know *what* will happen, we want to know *why*. This ability to evoke curiosity and empathy lies at the heart of story-telling.

Reading about writing can be a time-consuming experience. Most libraries or bookshops today have an array of books on literary and critical theory, as well as hands-on guides to writing fiction. The latter traditionally analyse the standard categories of plot and narrative, description, character, dialogue, point of view, and beginnings and endings. While technically invaluable—writing is a craft as well as an art—beware the implication that a novel can be dissected like a specimen on a laboratory table, and writing 'learned' by following a set of guidelines.

To deepen your appreciation of fiction, read as widely and as well as possible, acquiring a sensitivity to various texts as well as an understanding of the literary strategies of their writers and prevailing critical opinion. Don't lose sight of the fact that there are as many ways of writing as there are books in a bookshop, and that while literary criticism is obliged to pick novels apart, in a successful novel all aspects work together seamlessly to create the whole.

Take description, character and dialogue, for instance. Descriptive prose blends with dialogue; characters are defined by their choice of words and manner of speech as much as by their actions:

'I don't see,' said the Queen, 'why there is any need for a press release at all. Why should the public care what I am reading? The Queen reads. That is all they need to know. "So what?" I imagine the general response.'

'To read is to withdraw. To make oneself unavailable. One would feel easier about it,' said Sir Kevin, 'if the pursuit itself were less... selfish.'

'Selfish?'

'Perhaps I should say solipsistic.'

'Perhaps you should.'

Sir Kevin plunged on. 'Were we able to harness your reading to some larger purpose—the literacy of the nation as a whole, for instance, the improvement of reading standards among the young...'

'One reads for pleasure,' said the Queen. 'It is not a public duty.'

'Perhaps,' said Sir Kevin, 'it should be.'

'Bloody cheek,' said the duke when she told him that night.

A Bennett, *The Uncommon Reader*, Faber and Faber, London, 2007, pp. 45–6

'Zofia is going to make bolls,' Edek said. 'There are no bolls in New York. No bolls what are good, I mean. There are a few such Italian bolls but there is not one boll shop.'

Zofia and Walentyna looked expectantly at Ruth.

'What is a boll shop?' Ruth said.

'A shop what does sell bolls, off coss,' said Edek.

'And what are bolls?' Ruth said.

All three of them looked at her. They looked at her both in amazement, and as though she was retarded.

> 'Ruthie, are you stupid?' Edek said. 'You do know off coss what is a boll. Everybody does know what is a boll.' Edek was agitated. 'Even a person what does not eat bolls, what does eat such food with leafs like you, does know what is a boll,' he said.
>
> 'I don't eat leaves,' said Ruth. 'I eat a variety of fruit and vegetables and grains and fish and non–fat dairy products, and sometimes chicken. I eat a pretty healthy diet.'
>
> 'Pheh!' Edek said. 'You do eat food what is not normal.'
>
> 'Edek, Ruthie is right. The food she does eat is very good,' Zofia said, patting Edek on the head.
>
> Ruth, too, was now agitated. And perplexed. Why did Edek have to bring up her eating habits? And what was a boll?
>
> 'A boll is a boll what is made from meat,' Edek said.
>
> 'Oh, a meatball,' said Ruth.
>
> 'Yes, a meatball,' Zofia and Walentyna half shouted with a degree of relief.
>
> L Brett, *You Gotta Have Balls*, Picador, Sydney, 2005, p. 142

Both passages are notable for their accomplished dialogue and comical flair, but how different they are! The first passage is marked by restraint, understatement and a very careful verbal sparring as Sir Kevin dares to question the Queen's flippant—as he sees it—analysis of reading as largely a private and enjoyable activity.

The second passage verges on the farcical, using deliberate repetition and an emphasis on accented and grammatically idiosyncratic language as Polish-born Edek openly ridicules his daughter's edgy, inner-city, quasi-vegetarianism.

Descriptive passages vary as much as dialogue, depending on point of view and to what degree the writer wants us to identify with a character—in these cases, victims of a crime:

> The corpse was that of a young woman, slim and yellow-haired; she had been pretty, but death had robbed her of her features and now she might be a carving in soapstone, primitive and bland. Something, his pathologist's instinct perhaps, told him what the name would be before he looked at the label tied to her toe. 'Christine Falls,' he murmured. 'You were well named.' Looking more closely he noticed the dark roots of her hair at forehead and temples: dead, and not even a real blonde.
>
> B Black, *Christine Falls*, Picador, Sydney, 2006, p. 10

> The girl, about fifteen or sixteen by the look of her, lay on her back in the long grass behind a huge Victorian sepulchre, upon which stood a marble statue of an angel. The angel had its back turned to her, and through the fog Banks could make out the chipped feathers of its wings.
>
> Her eyes stared into the fog, her long blonde hair lay fanned out around her head like a halo, and her face had a reddish–purple hue. There was a little cut by her left eye and some discolouration around her neck. A trickle of blood the shape of a large teardrop ran out of her left nostril …
>
> P Robinson, *Innocent Graves*, Pan Books, London, 2003, pp. 3–4

Both passages deal with the death of a young, blonde girl. In the first passage, however, the pathologist Quirke resists the impulse to feel emotionally involved. His caustic observation that the girl was 'not even a real blonde' is, we recognise, an attempt to distance himself from the death at hand.

In the second passage, our empathy for the victim is, to the contrary, shaped by Inspector Banks' sense of tragedy, heightened by the fanciful suggestion that the angel had perhaps turned its back on the dead girl, and his likening her fanned-out hair to a halo, and the blood running from her nose to a large teardrop.

In both cases, however, our feelings are expertly manipulated: we identify more with Banks than Quirke, and share Banks' point of view to a greater extent than we do Quirke's.

Plain English

Broadly speaking, the short words are the best, and the old words, when short, are best of all.

Attributed to Sir Winston Churchill, British politician (1874–1965)

Clear thinking is the key to clear writing, and the basis of what is known today as Plain English. In fact, its values were advocated by the likes of George Orwell and Sir Ernest Gowers long before the term 'Plain English' was coined in the UK in 1979. What began as a reaction against prevailing officialese turned into a widespread campaign to draw together the principles of good writing, and is now formally accepted as the foundation of written and spoken expression in academia, industry and government. Equivalent plain language campaigns are rapidly being adopted in other countries.

Why did language become so 'unplain' in the first place? Interestingly, obfuscation brought its own advantage: lawyers in medieval Europe discovered that the more words they used, the greater the fee they could charge—a practice which naturally encouraged lengthy, pompous and obscure expression. Once established, the habit became hard to break and inflated writing became for many a reassuring symbol of status. More recently, an 'official style' characterised language in bureaucracies, where expressions of individuality—as they were often regarded—incurred their own risk, and company statements had as much to do with increasing the perceived dignity of the business as informing the public of their products.

Even today, despite the shorthand language employed in Facebook, Twitter and other social media platforms as well as emails and text messages, we often mask precise facts or feelings in opaque expressions, and may find long, complicated sentences easier to write than short, clear ones.

Above all, make sure that your thoughts themselves are clear. As an anonymous diplomat once astutely observed, 'what appears to be a sloppy or meaningless use of words may well be a completely correct use of words to express sloppy or meaningless ideas' (quoted in Gowers 1986: 38).

There are many resources available on Plain English. All recommend that you create a clear and simple message that your reader or listener can easily understand. This doesn't mean that all subtlety should be filtered out from your writing, or personal style eradicated, but rather that your thoughts be clear and their expression simple and stylish. The layout and design of your text, including the typography, should enhance the communicability of your message.

Here is a summary of 10 'golden rules' for writing in Plain English.

1 Use everyday words

Use simple, informal language. This applies to individual words (e.g. 'start' *not* 'commence'; 'buy' *not* 'purchase'; and 'use' *not* 'utilise') as well as to phrases (e.g. 'can' *not* 'has the capacity to'; 'now' *not* 'at this point in time'; and 'if' *not* 'in the event'). For example:

> If there is a delay, please use the second lounge

is simpler than

> In the event of a delay, please utilise the second lounge.

If you're unsure about the value of a word or phrase, try omitting it to see if it has any effect. For example:

He drew attention to himself by the fact that he was boasting about his travels

is perfectly clear when 'the fact that' is removed:

He drew attention to himself by boasting about his travels.

Again:

Lessons begin the week commencing Monday 19th February

can be condensed to

Lessons begin the week of Monday 19th February.

Guard against tautologies (i.e. the useless repetition of the same idea or meaning in different words). For example:

I urge you to cut out the unnecessary padding

can become

I urge you to cut out the padding.

Unless you're writing poetry or deliberately recreating the diction of a particular era or location, avoid archaic phrases (e.g. use 'while' *not* 'whilst'; 'see' *not* 'behold'; and 'from now on' *not* 'henceforth').

Resist using foreign phrases where English equivalents do just as well (e.g. 'face-to-face' *not* 'vis-à-vis; 'instead of' *not* 'in lieu of'; and 'a year' *not* 'per annum').

Foreign phrases are, however, perfectly acceptable when there is no precise English counterpart (which is why words like 'hotel' were imported in the first place and so fully absorbed into English that their foreign derivation is largely forgotten). For example, the phrase *laissez faire*, literally 'let (them) act' is more efficient than referring to 'an approach of non-interference in or indifference to the affairs of others'. In the political sense of a 'laissez-faire economy' the phrase is again more concise than 'an economy in which the government involves itself as little as possible'.

Foreign phrases are also acceptable when the closest equivalent lacks the same vigour or feeling. For example, we all know what is meant by 'the good life', but it doesn't have the ring of *la dolce vita*, nor the connotation. Again, in a poetic context, a 'bunch' of flowers doesn't work as well as a 'bouquet' of flowers.

2 Avoid jargon and euphemisms

Resist jargon and pretentious euphemisms (e.g. 'attitude' rather than 'mindset', and 'communication' or 'contact' rather than 'interface'). Even words whose original meanings are precise can become stale through overuse (e.g. 'initiate', 'facilitate' and 'implement') and are best replaced by simple words (e.g. 'start', 'help' or 'carry out'). Others are used so universally and indiscriminately that they are usually best left out altogether (e.g. 'absolutely', 'basically' and 'literally').

The tendency towards verbosity afflicts language everywhere. No wonder that current euphemisms are ready targets for satire! For example:

> high-net-worth-individuals (i.e. the rich)
>
> economically-challenged (i.e. the poor)

In academia, for instance, straightforward ideas are often dressed up as sophisticated concepts. For example:

> With the attainment of self-actualisation, the development of talent becomes an end in itself

can be shrunk to

> Developing your talent can become an end in itself.

Here, the term 'self-actualisation'—which refers to the realising of a person's potential to develop as a fulfilled individual—is of debatable value. If you're 'developing your talent', a degree of self-realisation (or self-knowledge) is implied. 'The attainment of' serves only to compound an already nebulous situation.

In industry, the purpose of language may differ but its expression can be equally obscure. The meaning behind company mission statements and official correspondence is often veiled and difficult to extract. For example:

> Terminating the marginal employee may be necessary if all steps of the company's conflict resolution policy with regard to the employee have been exhausted

leaves us exhausted too. All it means is:

> We have to fire people if they are not doing their job properly and if our conflict resolution policy hasn't worked.

If this sounds abrasive, careful use of a passive can shift the emphasis on to the employee rather than the firing, and soften the tone without clouding the meaning:

> Employees who are not performing their job satisfactorily, and whom our conflict resolution policy has not assisted, will be asked to leave.

Jargon and euphemism may be rife where we might least expect it—in general information for the wider public such as community notices, menus and the like. This heading, for example, in an otherwise immaculately produced brochure, reads:

> The guide aims to meet the information needs of clients

which, simply put, means

> The guide aims to answer clients' questions.

Again, a cautionary line to students about to take an exam asks them to:

> Please keep verbal input concise

rather than following its own advice, and saying

> Please be concise.

3 Minimise figures of speech

A figure of speech is an expression in which words are used in a non-literal sense to suggest an image or to achieve a particular effect. The most common figures of speech are similes and metaphors. Similes express a direct resemblance of one thing to another, and usually start with 'as' or 'like' (from the Latin *similis*, meaning 'like'). Metaphors go a step further by expressing a resemblance by directly equating one thing with another (from the Greek *metaphora*, meaning 'a transfer'). To simplify: similes say one thing is *like* another; metaphors say it *is* another.

Use similes and metaphors sparingly. Make sure that they are still evocative, and not 'dead', as George Orwell called those that have lost their original effect and become merely a device for lazy thinking. For example:

> The noise rippled through the crowd like breeze through long grass

is an effective simile because noise is not normally associated with the rippling effect of wind through grass, whereas

> The victim said that her legs felt as heavy as lead

has little impact because the phrase 'as heavy as lead' is already so familiar. Again,

> The thoughts hammered at her mind, making sleep impossible

is a vivid metaphor because the image of thoughts hammering is unusual, whereas

> The man is a lion—he is courageous, strong and will do anything to defend himself!

is less effective because brave, strong men described as lions is, by now, a cliché.

At the other end of the scale avoid overblown expressions that, while original, risk being absurd. This caption, for example, describing a World Youth Day mass

> It was a tsunami of faith and joy

conjures up images of aquatic devastation—presumably not the desired effect.

Also avoid mixed metaphors (i.e. combining incompatible or incongruous images to express one concept). For example:

> I'm really cheesed off by having to eat humble pie.

Closely connected with metaphors are idioms (in the sense of phrases that convey non-literal meanings that cannot be inferred from their individual words). Like metaphors, idioms must retain their ability to surprise. By becoming common, they lose the maverick quality that makes them idiomatic (from the Greek *idios*, meaning 'private, peculiar or strange'). For example:

> The child was so excited that he let the cat out of the bag

is a lively idiom because it makes us picture a cat springing from a bag, whereas

> The joke had been done to death

has little effect because the expression to 'do to death' has itself been killed—or is at least languishing—through overuse. Such expressions are best replaced by strong verbs, which are often more precise. This last line could therefore be rephrased:

> The joke had been already made (or heard) so many times.

The etymology of idioms makes entertaining—and informative—reading. By far the richest sources of English idioms are the Bible and Shakespeare. About some origins we can take an educated guess: 'To wash your hands of something' dates from the action of Pontius

Pilate before surrendering to the crowd and handing Christ over to be crucified.

The origin of others is less obvious: 'Salad days' was first used by Shakespeare, when Cleopatra refers to her youth when she was 'green in judgment' (*Antony and Cleopatra*, Act 1, Scene 5, ll. 67–75).

Still others have diverse origins: 'To let the cat out of the bag' recalls the practice of unscrupulous medieval merchants of selling a cat in a bag rather than another more valuable animal so that the unsuspecting customer, untying it later, would literally let the cat out of the bag.

4 Avoid turning nouns into verbs

In most cases, resist turning nouns into verbs. Note that 'verbing' is more accepted in American English where brand names too make a frequent appearance. For example:

> Please hoover the floor while I xerox the document

would take the place of

> Please vacuum the floor while I photocopy the document.

Nevertheless, as a general rule, avoid turning nouns into verbs. Although few would quibble with 'televise' being created from 'television', or 'trivialise' from 'trivial', beware the invasion on both sides of the Atlantic of the so-called 'new verbs' where brevity is achieved at the cost of style with no extra clarity.

Sometimes a noun is lifted out intact, and inserted in a sentence as a verb. For example:

> The decision will impact the market

is less elegant than

> The decision will have an impact on the market.

Another common example is:

> You may need to action this

which again is less stylish than

> You may need to take action on this.

At other times a noun is truncated, and its root used as a verb. For example:

> We will process down the aisle

is a mangled version of

> We will have a procession (or proceed) down the aisle.

Most common of all, '-ise' (or its accompanying '-isation') is added at the end of a noun and the new word treated as a verb. For example:

> Please diarise these dates

competes with the simpler though slightly more wordy

> Please put these dates in your diary.

Even when an '-ise' word is fully acceptable, its '-isation' version rarely offers an advantage, and makes a sentence unwieldy. For example:

> Prioritisation of tasks is critical in management

is more awkward than

> Prioritising (or the ability to prioritise) tasks is critical in management.

Avoid the related tendency to add '-ful' at the end of a noun to turn it into an adjective. This usually offers no advantage, literary or otherwise. For example:

> The film was suspenseful, the documentary insightful

is clumsier than

> The film was full of suspense, the documentary perceptive.

Clearly, shorter is not necessarily clearer.

5 Use the active voice

Favour the active over the passive voice, and the subject–verb–object sentence construction. For example:

> You can download the magazine at any time

is simpler and more friendly than

> The magazine can be downloaded at any time.

Again, this sentence:

> Do not place material in a way that blocks pedestrian and vehicle access

is easier to absorb than

> Material must not be placed in a way that blocks pedestrian and vehicle access.

Sometimes, however, the passive voice is desirable. For example, to alter the emphasis:

> Internet banking can be used to pay invoices

(where the focus is Internet banking rather than the invoices)

or to make words less confrontational:

> Prompt payment would be greatly appreciated

(less hostile than 'please pay immediately')

or if the 'doer' is unknown:

> The new site has had over 1000 hits.

6 Address the reader as 'you'

Address both general readers and business clients as 'you' which is both friendly and direct. (Imagine that the person you're addressing is sitting opposite you.) In doing so, you can often drop the passive voice. For example:

> The centre encourages you to participate

is less intimidating than

> Client participation is encouraged by the centre.

If you're speaking on behalf of an organisation, use 'we'. Again, this is friendlier as it avoids creating a sense of 'us' and 'them'. The example above could therefore be further improved:

> We encourage you to participate.

Sometimes the 'us' and 'them' approach is deliberately used to invoke a sense of urgency or authority on the part of the organisation. As a strategy, its success is questionable: does a direct appeal to the reader necessarily erode the speaker's authority? For example:

> If you don't register now, we cannot guarantee your entry in the competition

is as forceful as

> The Academy cannot guarantee entry in the competition unless registration is received now

although markedly less friendly than

> Register with us now to guarantee your entry in the competition.

7 Keep sentences short and tenses consistent

Make sentences succinct. Each sentence should contain one main point, and each paragraph one main theme. Experts suggest that 15–20 words is an ideal length for the average sentence, but obviously this is a very general guide and variety is critical. While long sentences and complex grammatical constructions are hard to understand, too rapid a succession of short, sharp sentences may be equally indigestible.

This paragraph, for example, though it consists of four short sentences that in themselves are clear, quickly loses our interest:

> There are nearly 400 public libraries in the state. They range from being old and in need of a revamp to brand-new and cutting edge. Libraries today are a focal point for the local community. They are exciting without being daunting, fun yet functional, and accessible to all.

The same information, presented in two overly long sentences, is no better:

> There are nearly 400 public libraries in the state, in every stage of development from old and in need of a revamp to brand-new and cutting edge. Libraries today are a focal point for the local community as they are exciting without being daunting, fun yet functional, and accessible to all.

Yet this version, which blends short lines with longer ones, is fluid and easy to understand:

> There are nearly 400 public libraries in the state. They range from being old and in need of a revamp to brand-new and cutting edge. Libraries today are a focal point for the local community—exciting without being daunting, fun yet functional, and accessible to all.

The tense used can affect the length of a sentence, too. Above all, keep the tense consistent. It is easy to slip into the past or future tense, but the present is usually the most appropriate and invariably more succinct. For example:

> All artworks are chosen by specialists

is neater than

> All artworks have been chosen by specialists.

Again:

> Avoid direct sunlight as it accelerates the process of degradation

is preferable to

> Avoid direct sunlight as it will accelerate the process of degradation.

8 Be specific and concrete

Refer to the specific rather than the universal, and to the concrete rather than the abstract. Name a particular object or activity rather than a process or technique. Use straightforward verbs rather than nominalisations; that is, abstract nouns that are formed from verbs (e.g. 'to provide' rather than 'the provision of', and 'to investigate' rather than 'carry out an investigation of'). For example:

> The school is committed to providing quality education for all students

is more succinct than

> The school is committed to the provision of quality education for all students.

As it is difficult to provide something as long-term as education without a prior commitment, the sentence can be pared down further:

> The school provides quality education for all students.

Again:

> An elite police team is investigating recent crimes in the area

is better than

> An elite police team is carrying out an investigation into recent crimes in the area.

9 Be definite

Be positive, not negative. Assert what you believe the situation is rather than suggest what you think it might not be. For example:

> Write neatly if you want people to understand you

is stronger than

> Don't write so messily or people might not be able to understand you.

Avoid the 'not un-' construction which makes most sentences both longer and indefinite. For example:

> I am grateful for your advice

is more direct than

> I am not ungrateful for your advice

although the resulting vagueness, like the use of passives and filler words, may be an unconscious effort to make what follows more palatable:

> I am not ungrateful for your advice, but will still take out a court order against her.

Do not overuse qualifiers (e.g. 'really', 'very' and 'rather'). For example:

> I feel queasy so will not attend the ceremony

is crisper than

> I feel really very queasy so would rather not attend the ceremony.

If this is too crisp, the phrase can be modified to

> I feel queasy so prefer not to attend the ceremony

(although being less definite, this includes the possibility that the speaker may attend).

Do not over-qualify whole sentences. For example:

> If you contact us at the end of the year, we will confirm availability of the tour

is more accurate than

> If you would like to contact us at the end of the year, we can confirm availability of the tour

(unless you wish to allow for the possibility that the speaker could confirm availability of the tour but will not necessarily do so!).

Reserve a degree of doubt or hesitation for when it is essential, or—in fiction—characterises the speaker. In the hands of the most skilful writers, deliberate use of 'not' and even the double negative achieve precision of thought as well as elegance. For example:

> I speak not to disprove what Brutus spoke,
> But here I am to speak what I do know.
>
> Shakespeare, *Julius Caesar*, Act 3, Scene 2, ll. 156–7

10 Revise, revise, revise!

None of us is immune from error. When you're sure you've finished your manuscript, spend some time re-reading it, preferably after a brief interval away.

If possible, have others read it through too: each fresh set of eyes brings with it a fresh perspective.

Perhaps nothing reminds us better of the importance of checking our own words than the comical errors of others.

> Don't send your answer to the college as this activity is to encourage you to think about 'quality'.
>
> Advice in student course notes

> If you are specifically interested in alcohol or drugs, go to the site below.
>
> Line from a health information service website

> Special offer on desert wine—today only!
>
> Placard in liquor store

> If the water is off when you turn it on, please turn it on again.
>
> Notice in an Italian public lavatory, 1950s

* * *

The principles of Plain English are useful pointers to successful writing but, like all rules, they must be applied thoughtfully and with respect to the wider context. Good grammar and syntax without style does not make for fluid writing any more than notes correctly composed make a symphony.

Commonly misused words

Words are the source of misunderstandings.

Antoine de Saint-Exupéry, The Little Prince *(published 1943), Chapter XXI*

When a particular turn of phrase is heard often enough, even though grammatically incorrect, it is apt to be accepted.

Does it really matter? 'But everyone knows what I mean!' is the standard defence of sloppy language. Not so: in a poorly composed sentence this may only hold true in a general sense while precise shades of meaning are lost.

Among the words that are prone to being misused there is a persistent cluster that appears both in written and spoken form. Some words have multiple meanings depending on whether they are used as verbs (transitive or intransitive) or nouns; others are simply confused with words that have similar sound patterns and are frequently spelled the same, but have different meanings (i.e. homonyms). Pronouns, too, often cause confusion.

Here is a list of frequently misused words, together with their most common definitions. For more details, refer to the *Macquarie Dictionary* which sets the standard for Australian English.

Affect/effect

'To affect' means to influence or act upon, either positively or adversely. For example:

His generosity affected me deeply.

Her reckless behaviour severely affected me.

It can also mean to feign or make a pretence of something, particularly an emotion. For example:

With her mourning outfit and bowed head she affected great sorrow, but few trusted her.

An 'effect' is a result or consequence. For example:

The seizure of their father had an overwhelming effect on the children.

'To effect' means to bring about. For example:

Let us do everything we can to effect his release.

Aggravate/irritate

'To aggravate' means to make worse or intensify a matter or condition. For example:

Riding my bicycle aggravated my ankle sprain.

'To irritate' means to annoy or exasperate. For example:

I was irritated that I was not allowed to ride my bicycle for six weeks.

Alternate/alternative

'To alternate' means to occur successively or by turns; as an adjective, it means every other. For example:

Day and night alternate.

They play golf on alternate weekends.

An 'alternative' is a choice, especially between two things or courses of action. For example:

You may walk; the alternative is to drive.

Assure/ensure/insure

'To assure' means to convince or cause a person to feel certain or sure. For example:

> She assured him that she had protected her valuables.

'To ensure' means to make certain or sure. For example:

> He ensured that his policy would arrive safely by delivering it in person.

Note that in American English 'ensure' is sometimes spelled 'insure'.

'To insure' means to guarantee or protect against loss or damage. For example:

> They insured their valuables against theft for $30 000.

Complement/compliment

A 'complement' means that which completes or makes perfect; 'to complement' carries the equivalent meaning. For example:

> The pictures are a complement to the text.

> Pictures and text complement each other.

A 'compliment' refers to an expression of praise or admiration; again, 'to compliment' has an equivalent meaning. For example:

> I received an unexpected compliment.

> I must compliment you on your choice of colours.

Comprise/constitute

'To comprise' means to consist of (i.e. of all the parts). Note that it should *not* be followed by 'of'. For example:

> The jury comprises various people
> *not* the jury comprises of various people.

Less precisely, it is used in the sense of to include or contain (i.e. some, but not necessarily all, of the parts). For example:

> The jury comprises my neighbour.

'To constitute' means to compose, form or make up. For example:

> The people who constitute the jury come from a variety of backgrounds.

Desert/dessert

A 'desert' is an arid, barren and mostly uninhabited expanse of land. For example:

> The Sahara Desert is larger than Australia.

'To desert' means to abandon or forsake. For example:

> She deserted her friends for the sake of her children.

A 'dessert' is the sweet dish served at the end of a meal. For example:

> For dessert we were offered fresh dates, honey cake, and stuffed apricots.

Note that in the phrase 'to get your just deserts', meaning to get what you deserve be it reward or punishment, 'deserts' is spelled like the former but pronounced like the latter (it derives from the French *deservir*, meaning 'to deserve'). For example:

> The gangsters were robbed at knifepoint? Well, they got their just deserts!

Disinterested/uninterested

'Disinterested' means impartial or unbiased. For example:

> Let a disinterested teacher monitor the rivalry between the students.

'Uninterested' means not interested in. For example:

> The students were uninterested in their lesson.

Enjoy/enthuse

'To enjoy!' is a transitive verb (i.e. we must enjoy *something*), though used as a common exhortation in the wider sense of having a good time. For example:

> The tour of the castle starts now. Enjoy!

is more correctly expressed as

> The tour of the castle starts now. Enjoy it!

'To enthuse' is an example of the opposite: an intransitive verb (meaning to feel or show enthusiasm) often treated as a transitive one (meaning to cause enthusiasm in). For example:

> He was enthused by the talk

is more properly expressed as

> The talk gave him much to enthuse about

or by turning it into an adjective, as in

> He was enthusiastic about the talk.

Good/well

'Good' is an adjective; 'well' is an adverb. For example:

> The food tastes good.
>
> I feel well.

Avoid using 'good' as an adverb unless you're writing dialogue to capture colloquialisms—or unless you mean well-behaved.

He/she and him/her

'He' and 'she' refer to the subjects of a sentence; 'him' and 'her' refer to the objects. For example:

> He and she are good friends.
>
> She is good friends with him.

Errors can creep in when, like the author of this newspaper headline, we attempt a more dramatic turn of phrase and lose sight of subject and object:

> Betrayed, by she who provided hope!

instead of

> Betrayed, by her who provided hope!

If a line that is grammatically correct sounds awkward, it can usually be rephrased. The one above, for example, could read:

> Betrayed, by the person who provided hope!

Historic/historical

'Historic' means what is recorded or noted down in history, and is also used more loosely to cover what is considered significant or famous in history. For example:

> Hannibal's crossing of the Alps in 218 BC was truly an historic event.

'Historical' refers to something that actually happened in the past. For example:

> That the outbreak of Black Death in fourteenth-century Europe killed a third of its population is an historical fact.

I/me/myself

'I' refers to the subject of the sentence. For example:

I bought a ticket to the play for Danny.

Danny and I went to see the play.

'Me' refers to the object of the sentence. For example:

Danny said that the play was inspirational for him and for me.

'Myself' is usually used as a reflexive pronoun (i.e. one where the subject and object are the same), or as the emphatic form of 'I' or 'me'. For example:

I bandaged myself up after the accident.

I myself would never cut a red light!

Imply/infer

'To imply' means to suggest or indicate. For example:

The suitcases stacked at the front door imply that they were about to leave.

'To infer' means to deduce by reasoning. For example:

From the suitcases stacked at the front door, we infer that they were about to leave.

Lay/lie

'To lay' (past tense 'laid) means to put or place down (as distinct from colloquial use of the noun 'lay'). For example:

If they lay their work out on the table, they will see it more clearly.

'To lie' has two meanings: first, to tell lies ('lied' is the past tense) and second, to lie down horizontally ('laid' is the past tense). For example:

If he lies about his results again, I will have to see his teacher.

She likes to lie down on the sofa with the TV on to do her revision.

Like

'Like' peppers conversations everywhere, often ungrammatically. Its most common correct usage is as a verb (meaning to find agreeable) or as a preposition governing nouns or pronouns (meaning similar to). For example:

> I like vanilla ice-cream.
>
> This ice-cream is like the one I had on holiday.

'Like' tends to be misused in three main ways. First, it should not be used in place of the conjunction 'as'. For example:

> He looked like he wanted that ice-cream

is best expressed

> He looked as if he wanted that ice-cream.

Note that using 'like' as a conjunction is acceptable in colloquial speech, as well as in written form in American English.

Second, when used as a filler, 'like' is vague and suggests an unwillingness, or inability, to commit to a clear unequivocal statement. Like 'sort of' or 'kind of' (expressions which it often accompanies) it is best avoided. For example:

> She said that too much ice-cream is, like, bad for you

implies that 'she' is not sure whether an excessive amount of ice-cream is bad for us or not, or that she is being deliberately coy. This can be simplified to

> She said that too much ice-cream is bad for you.

Third, 'like' should never be used to replace a verb that expresses saying or demonstrating. For example:

> We were, like, 'Let's go to the movies!' But she was, like, 'I don't want to'

is confusing as well as inelegant. Did 'she' actually express a desire not to go to the movies, or is the speaker inferring it from her manner or a gesture? The sentence can be rephrased in various ways, depending on what took place. For example:

> We wanted to go to the movies, but she didn't want to

or, ideally, by being more precise:

> We suggested going to the movies, but she refused

or by reproducing the actual exchange of words:

> We said, 'Let's go to the movies,' but she said, 'I don't want to.'

Loose/lose

'Loose', the adjective, means free or released from constraint, often in the sense of not being tightly compacted. For example:

> He complained that his wallet was full of loose change.

'To lose' means to part with or mislay. For example:

> He loses his wallet regularly.

May/might

The verb 'may' is usually used to express a high degree of probability or possibility, or permission or opportunity. It is also used to express a strong wish or desire; to convey purpose or result in clauses introduced by 'that' or 'so that'; and to indicate ability or capacity politely and with a degree of closeness, especially in questions. For example:

> She may be right. (*high probability*)

> You may enter after 3.00 pm. (*permission*)

> Long may he live! (*wish*)

> Write it down so that future generations may understand. (*purpose*)

> May I assist you? (*polite question*)

The verb 'might' expresses a lesser degree of probability or possibility, or more uncertainty. It is also the past tense or subjunctive mood of 'may', conveying a greater remoteness in both time and probability, and often a lingering regret. It also expresses advisability, as well as a greater deference and formality than 'may', 'ought' or 'should', especially in questions. For example:

She might be right. (*less probability*)

I might have won the trophy. (*past tense of 'may'*)

He might at least acknowledge me! (*advisability*)

Might I assist you? (*polite formal question)*

The difference between 'may' and 'might', though subtle, is worth preserving: the modern tendency of opting for 'may' can have a flattening effect, as well as resulting in ungrammatical sentences. For example:

Who knows what might have happened?

is more speculative, and richer in possibilities, than

Who knows what may have happened?

(which is also ungrammatical).

Practice/practise

A 'practice' refers to a regular habit or custom, or a business. For example:

Serena makes a practice of thanking people profusely if they help her.

She drops into the doctor's practice regularly to show her gratitude.

'To practise' means to carry out or perform, or do habitually; the adjective 'practised' means experienced. For example:

Victor's practising for his performance again!

At this rate, he will be a practised concert pianist by the time he is nine!

Note that in American English both noun and verb are spelled 'practice'.

Principal/principle

A 'principal' is the highest person in rank or importance. For example:

Opinion is divided on the new principal.

As an adjective, it means main or chief. For example:

My principal reason for moving here is to send my children to this school.

A 'principle' is a rule of conduct or ethical standard. For example:

She is widely respected for her strong principles.

That/which

'That' is a defining, or restrictive, pronoun (i.e. one that defines the noun with essential, specific information). For example:

The piano that she wanted is in the corner of the showroom.

'Which' is a non-defining, or non-restrictive, pronoun (i.e. one that adds non-essential information, in the nature of a comment). Its purpose is parenthetic, with the additional information enclosed within a pair of commas.

The piano, which was made in Japan, is in the corner of the showroom.

The commas are important. If they are in the wrong place, or absent, the sentence can become ambiguous. For example:

All baggage belonging to sports teams, that are travelling to Bangkok, will be checked by security implies that baggage belonging to all sports teams will be checked, whether or not that team is travelling to Bangkok, whereas

> All baggage belonging to sports teams that are travelling to Bangkok will be checked by security

leaves us in no doubt that only the baggage of Bangkok-bound sports teams will be checked by security.

That/who

'That' applies to inanimate objects; 'who' applies to people. For example:

> If there are any books that need to be covered, please leave them on the desk.
>
> If there are any volunteers who could help cover them, it would be much appreciated.

The pronouns 'that' and 'who' are frequently misplaced, as in this newsletter written, regrettably, by a librarian:

> If there are any volunteers that could help cover books, it would be much appreciated.

Who/whom

'Who' refers to the subject (i.e. a subjective pronoun). For example:

> the woman who runs the company, and the refugees who arrived yesterday
>
> (i.e. she runs the company, and they arrived yesterday.)

It is also used to frame questions. For example:

> Who is coming to the party? Who told her about it?
>
> (i.e. Is he/she coming to the party? Did he/she tell her about it?)

'Whom' refers to the object (i.e. an objective pronoun). For example:

> Whom did you ask? To whom did you give the parcel?

(i.e. Did you ask him/her? Did you give the parcel to him/her?)

'Whom' is being edged out by 'who', especially in conversation. Instead of the phrases above, for example, we might hear:

Who did you ask? Who did you give the parcel to?

Despite its increasingly formal overtones, the who/whom distinction is worth observing as it serves a grammatical purpose. It also avoids dangling prepositions—though, as Churchill famously demonstrated, sticking rigidly to their avoidance can result in absurdity:

This is the type of errant pedantry up with which I will not put.

Avoid incorrect uses of 'whom', in particular mistaking subject for object and therefore using the objective form. For example:

the singer whom Thomas argued had been vilified

should read

the singer who Thomas argued had been vilified

'who' being the subject of 'had been'. Again, if you're unsure, rephrasing the sentence using 'he', 'she' or 'they' immediately distinguishes subject from object (i.e. Thomas argued that *he/she* had been vilified).

Whose

The relative pronoun 'whose' (which means belonging to or relating to) applies equally to people and inanimate objects. For example:

the traveller whose car had been hit

the apartment whose décor was tasteful.

(Confusion arose because 'whose' used to be considered by grammarians to apply exclusively to people but this prejudice, which led to many an awkward sentence using 'of which', is now discarded.)

When used in a question, 'whose' only applies to people. For example:

> Whose speech do you prefer?
>
> At whose house will you stay?

Variant spellings

It's a damn poor mind that can think of only
one way to spell a word!

Andrew Jackson, seventh President of the United States (1767–1845), drafting a presidential paper

Differences in spellings between British and American English are much debated and the source of frequent confusion. American spelling is simpler and more phonetic than the British equivalent. In most Commonwealth countries and in Ireland, spelling conventions lean towards those of British English, whereas Canadian spelling is closer to American English—although in all English-speaking countries the American influence is increasingly felt.

If in doubt, refer to the latest edition of the appropriate dictionary. British English is usually based on the *Oxford English Dictionary*; and American English commonly refers to *Webster's Dictionary*. Regional variations are now also firmly establishing themselves: Australian English is based on the *Macquarie Dictionary*; New Zealand spelling uses the *New Zealand Oxford Dictionary*; Canadian spelling uses the *Canadian Oxford Dictionary*; and South African spelling uses the *Oxford South African Concise Dictionary*. (For full publishing details on dictionaries and other reference books, see the Bibliography.)

When using a spellchecker, make sure that you set it on the correct English language version.

Here is a list of common variants, the most confusing listed first.

- **'ise' or 'ize'?** For verbs ending in '-ise' or '-yse', British English uses 'ise' or 'yse' (e.g. authorise, organise/analyse, paralyse), whereas American English uses 'ize' or 'yze' (e.g. authorize, organize/analyze, paralyze).

  This difference also applies to corresponding nouns (e.g. authorisation, organisation/authorization, organization).

  Exception: Some words always end in '-ise' in both British and American English (e.g. advertise, advise, comprise, compromise, exercise, franchise, improvise, revise, supervise, surprise, televise).

- **'-our' or '-or'?** At the ends of words, British English uses '-our' (e.g. behaviour, colour, honour), whereas American English uses '-or' (e.g. behavior, color, honor).

  This difference also applies to derivative words (e.g. behavioural, colourful, honourable/behavioral, colorful, honorable).

  Exception: Some derivatives drop the 'u' in both British and American English (e.g. honorific, humorous, vigorous).

- **'-re' or '-er'?** At the ends of words, British English uses '-re' (e.g. centre, metre, theatre), whereas American English uses '-er' (e.g. center, meter, theater).

  Exception: Some words ending in '-cre' retain that ending in both British and American English (e.g. acre, massacre, mediocre).

- **'-ce' or '-se'?** At the ends of words, both British and American English distinguish between '-ce' for nouns (e.g. some advice, a device), and '-se' for verbs (e.g. to advise, to devise).

Exception: American English uses 'license' and 'practice' as both nouns and verbs, and uses 'defense' and 'pretense' as nouns.

- **'-ed' or '-t'?** For the past tense of verbs with alternative endings, both British and American English use '-ed' (e.g. burned, learned, spelled).

  Exception: British English also uses '-t' (e.g. burnt, learnt, spelt).

- **'-ement' or '-ment'?** At the ends of some nouns, British English uses '-ement' (e.g. abridgement, acknowledgement, judgement), whereas American English uses '-ment' (e.g. abridgment, acknowledgment, judgment).

- **'-eing' or '-ing'?** At the end of some verbs, British English uses '-eing' (e.g. ageing, bingeing, whingeing), whereas American English uses '-ing' (e.g. aging, binging, whinging).

- **'-eable' or '-able'?** When forming some adjectives, British English uses the suffix '-eable' (e.g. likeable, rateable, sizeable), whereas American English uses '-able' (e.g. likable, ratable, sizable).

  Exception: Some words are spelled the same in both British and American English (e.g. believable, curable, lovable, usable).

- **'-ll' or '-l'?** For words ending in the consonant 'l' that have a suffix beginning with a vowel, British English uses the double '-ll' (e.g. modelled, quarrelling, traveller), whereas American English uses the single '-l' (e.g. modeled, quarreling, traveler).

Where the suffix begins with a consonant and the word ends in 'l', however, British English retains the single 'l' (e.g. fulfilment, enrolment) but a word ending in a double 'll' loses an 'l' (e.g. instalment, skilful), whereas American English retains the double 'll' (e.g. fulfillment, enrollment, installment, skillful).

- **'-t' or '-tt'?** For words ending in the consonant 't' that have an unstressed final syllable and a suffix beginning with a vowel, both British English and American English use the single 't' (e.g. benefited, marketed, targeted).

  Exception: The word 'benefited' also appears as 'benefitted' in American English, and 'regretted' is spelled as such in both British English and American English.

- **'-ogue' or '-og'?** At the ends of some nouns, British English uses '-ogue' (e.g. catalogue, dialogue, synagogue), whereas American English uses '-og' (e.g. catalog, dialog, synagog).

  Exception: The word 'analog' also appears as 'analogue' in American English.

- **'-e', '-ae' or '-oe'?** In common words of classical origin, British English uses '-ae' and '-oe' (e.g. aesthetic, anaesthesia, encyclopaedia/amoeba, oestrogen, foetus), whereas American English uses '-e' (e.g. esthetic, anesthesia, encyclopedia, ameba, estrogen, fetus).

  Exception: Both British English and American English retain the composite or digraph vowels 'ae' and 'oe' in proper names (e.g. Caesar, Oedipus, Phoebe).

The table that follows offers a simplified summary of common points of difference:

British English	American English
-ise and **-yse** (e.g. organise, analyse)	**-ize** and **-yze** (e.g. organize, analyze)
-our (e.g. behaviour, colour, honour)	**-or** (e.g. behavior, color, honor)
-re (e.g. centre, metre, theatre)	**-er** (e.g. center, meter, theater)
-ce (e.g. defence, licence, practice) (*nouns*)	**-se** (e.g. defense, license, practise) (*nouns*)
-ed and **-t** (e.g. burned or burnt, spelled or spelt)	**-ed** (e.g. burned, spelled)
-ement (e.g. acknowledgement, judgement)	**-ment** (e.g. acknowledgment, judgment)
-eing (e.g. ageing, bingeing, whingeing)	**-ing** (e.g. aging, binging, whinging)
-eable (e.g. likeable, rateable, sizeable)	**-able** (e.g. likable, ratable, sizable)
-ll (e.g. modelled, quarrelled, travelled)	**-l** (e.g. modeled, quarreled, traveled)
-t (benefited, marketed, targeted)	**-t** and **-tt** (benefited or benefitted, marketed, targeted)
-ogue (e.g. catalogue, dialogue, synagogue)	**-og** (e.g. catalog, dialog, synagog)
-ae and **-oe** (e.g. aesthetic, amoeba)	**-e** (e.g. esthetic, ameba)

Note: These rules do not apply to quotes, where the author's original spelling and grammar—including any errors or idiosyncrasies—must be retained.

Nor do they apply to the names of organisations, which must be spelled as by the organisations themselves (e.g. Australian Lab**o**r Party *but* New Zealand Lab**ou**r Party).

British and American English

England and America are two countries divided by a common language.

Attributed to George Bernard Shaw, Irish playwright (1856–1950)

In vocabulary as in spelling, there are notable differences between British and American conventions. Thus, a Briton refers to the 'autumn' whereas an American refers to the 'fall'; the former uses 'petrol' whereas the latter uses 'gas'; and the former waits in a 'queue' whereas the latter waits in a 'line'. The former goes to the 'cinema' whereas the latter goes to the 'movies'; the former uses a 'mobile' whereas the latter uses a 'cell phone'; and the former takes out the 'rubbish' whereas the latter takes out the 'garbage'.

In idiomatic expressions, too, there are variations in the choice of words and their associations. Thus, the Briton 'touches wood' to bring luck whereas the American 'knocks on wood'; the former is 'out of line' whereas the latter is 'off base'; and the former says 'at the end of the day' whereas the latter says 'when all is said and done'.

Sometimes the difference between British English and American English lies in spelling and/or pronunciation alone. Thus, the Briton refers to 'aluminium' whereas the American refers to 'aluminum'; the former is 'sceptical' whereas the latter is 'skeptical'; and the former eats 'yoghurt' and wears 'pyjamas' whereas the latter eats 'yogurt' and wears 'pajamas'. Thanks largely to the informing power of the media and television and the pre-eminence of American programs, such variations barely cause a ripple in our general understanding.

When a difference lies in the actual words, however, confusion may arise. The wardrobe offers a delightfully rich repository for misunderstanding. Thus, the Briton puts on a 'dressing gown' whereas the American dons a 'bathrobe'; the former wears a 'jumper' whereas the latter wears a 'sweater' ('jumper' in America describes a dress with a blouse underneath such as in a girl's school uniform); and whereas the former might be invited to a 'fancy-dress party', the latter would attend a 'masquerade'.

Sometimes the difference between British and American English is further extended by regional variations. For example, Australian English often aligns itself with neither British English nor American English. Thus, an Australian wears 'gym shoes' or 'sandshoes' for sport whereas a Briton wears 'plimsolls' and an American wears 'sneakers'; an Australian wears a 'singlet' under a shirt or blouse whereas a Briton wears a 'vest' and an American wears an 'undershirt'; an Australian wears 'thongs' as summer footwear whereas a Briton wears 'flip-flops' and an American wears 'sandals'.

The potential for confusion and humour—or offence—increases with those words which are spelled the same and sound identical, yet whose meanings are culturally determined. Thus, 'fanny' in America is a light-hearted reference to one's bottom, whereas in Australia it is a derogatory term for a part of the female anatomy; 'pissed' is used colloquially to mean drunk in Britain or Australia, but means annoyed in America; and the above-mentioned 'thongs'—at least in the singular—in Britain refers to a G-string, in Australia refers to sandals, and in America can refer to both!

There are subtler differences in speech patterns too, reflected in grammar and syntax. Thus, British children are 'at' school, American children are 'in' school; a Briton lifts something 'off' the floor whereas an American lifts it 'off of' the floor; and a Briton 'writes to people' whereas an American 'writes people'.

Underlying the many semantic variations between British and American English is an essential difference in approach. American English is more assertive, colourful and elastic than British English, which at its best is more nuanced. Consider the differences in sense of humour: British comedy tends towards the ironic and self-deprecating; American comedy is bolder and more confrontational. As in vocabulary, regional variations fluctuate between the two: the Australian approach, for example, is less indirect than the British yet more laconic than the American.

Tricky singulars and plurals

Rarely is the question asked: Is our children learning?

George W Bush, campaigning in Florence, South Carolina, 11 January 2000

Practice rather than logic determines the spelling of many English plurals. Thus, 'piano' and 'radio' become 'pianos' and 'radios'; 'mosquito' and 'tomato' become 'mosquitoes' and 'tomatoes'; 'knife' and 'scarf' become 'knives' and 'scarves'; 'louse' and 'mouse' become 'lice' and 'mice'; 'basis' and 'crisis' become 'bases' and 'crises'; but 'aircraft', 'salmon' and 'sheep' remain unchanged.

With words of foreign derivation, the rules are if anything clearer.

Words of Latin and Greek origin

Most classically derived words that have become fully anglicised take the English ending 's' or 'es' when plural. This is not a clear-cut distinction, but rather a process in transition (e.g. 'cactuses' is edging out 'cacti' as the plural of 'cactus'; most dictionaries supply both, giving preference to the former). For example:

appendix *and* vortex (sing.) *become* appendixes *and* vortexes (pl.)

arena *and* formula (sing.) *become* arenas *and* formulas (pl.)

circus *and* referendum (sing.) *become* circuses *and* referendums (pl.)

Some words retain their original Latin plural ending because they are considered to be single entities composed of many parts (i.e. collective singulars). For example:

bacteria (e.g. the bacteria is deadly *not* the bacteria are deadly)

data (e.g. the data is complete *not* the data are complete)

media (e.g. the media is biased *not* the media are biased)

Those words ending in 'us' retain their original Latin plural ending because it is easier to pronounce than its English version (try saying 'nucleuses'). For example:

alumnus (sing.) *becomes* alumni (pl.)

nucleus (sing.) *becomes* nuclei (pl.)

stimulus (sing.) *becomes* stimuli (pl.)

Other everyday words that retain their original Latin plural ending include:

criterion (sing.) *becomes* criteria (pl.)

curriculum vitae (sing.) *becomes* curricula vitae (pl.)

phenomenon (sing.) *becomes* phenomena (pl.)

In scientific contexts, Latin words retain their original plural 'ae' ending. For example:

amoeba (sing.) *becomes* amoebae (pl.)

larva (sing.) *becomes* larvae (pl.)

vertebra (sing.) *becomes* vertebrae (pl.)

Words of French, Italian and Spanish origin

Words borrowed from any of the Romance languages (principally French, Italian and Spanish) that have become fully anglicised take the English ending 's' or 'es' when plural. For example:

bureau *and* tableau (sing.) *become* bureaus *and* tableaus (pl.)

fiasco *and* ghetto (sing.) *become* fiascos *and* ghettos (pl.)

paella *and* patio (sing.) *become* paellas *and* patios (pl.)

Again, in specialised contexts such as musical terminology, words borrowed from the Italian retain the original plural 'i' or 'e' ending. For example:

> concerti *not* concertos
>
> libretti *not* librettos
>
> maestri *not* maestros

Noun/verb agreement

Nouns and verbs in the same clause must agree with each other; that is, if a noun is singular, the verb must also be singular, and if a noun is plural, the verb must be too. Most of the time we observe this automatically and any errors are manifest, as in the quote at the beginning of this chapter.

In a long or complex sentence, however, when the verb becomes distanced from the noun to which it applies or associated with a different noun, errors may be less obvious. This conclusion to a report, for example, reads:

> The emphasis of the surveys that were commissioned to investigate the success of language programs were that more resources were needed to fund outreach activities.

Here, 'were' should read 'was' (or 'is'), because the main subject is the emphasis (singular) of the reports rather than the reports themselves (plural). Don't be distracted from the main subject, as this writer was by the plurality of the reports.

The rules become trickier with collective nouns that, depending on how they are used, may take singular or plural verbs.

Singular verbs

Collective nouns that emphasise the body as a whole take singular verbs (known as 'formal agreement'). For example:

The crowd is angry
not the crowd are angry.

This also applies to companies, organisations and the like when referred to collectively. For example:

Macy's is having a sale
not Macy's are having a sale.

Plural verbs

Collective nouns or names that emphasise the individual members take plural verbs (known as 'notional agreement'). For example:

The committee were unable to reach a unanimous decision
not the committee was unable to reach a unanimous decision
(*but* a committee was appointed to explore solutions).

* * *

Some words regularly cause confusion over whether they are singular or plural.

and...

Nouns joined by 'and' (i.e. 'compound subjects') take a plural verb. For example:

Health, wealth and security are her concern
not health, wealth and security is her concern

except when the nouns are so closely associated that they could be hyphenated. For example:

The scarf and glasses look is in fashion (*or* the scarf-and-glasses look is in fashion)
not the scarf and glasses look are in fashion.

If the subject is singular, and part of a sentence is enclosed parenthetically by two dashes and introduced by the word 'and', it takes a singular verb. For example:

> The lead actor—and his wife—is due (*or* the lead actor and his wife are due)
> *not* the lead actor—and his wife—are due.

each

Meaning 'each one', this is singular, and so it takes a singular verb. For example:

> Each boy has his own tutor *or* each boy has a tutor to himself.

For the sake of gender equality (and to avoid clumsy references to 'his or her'), 'each' can be followed by a plural pronoun. For example:

> Each traveller has their own cabin
> *rather than* each traveller has his or her own cabin.

either/or and neither/nor

Where both subjects are singular, 'either/or' and 'neither/nor' take singular verbs. For example:

> Either the teacher or the student is guilty.
>
> Neither my lens nor my camera is here.

If the subjects are mixed (i.e. singular and plural), the one closest to the verb determines whether the verb should be singular or plural. For example:

> Either the teacher or the students are guilty.
>
> Neither my lenses nor my camera is here.

everybody/everyone

Both take singular verbs. For example:

> How is everybody?
>
> Everyone is enjoying the carnival.

Again, for gender equality and neater expression, 'everybody' and 'everyone' can be followed by plural pronouns although rephrasing the sentence is preferable. For example:

Would everybody please take their seats? *or* would all guests please take their seats?
rather than would everybody please take his or her seats?

Everyone must carry their own bags *or* all travellers must carry their own bags
rather than everyone must carry his or her own bags.

Note that if they are written as separate words (i.e. 'every body', 'every one'), each word retains its separate meaning. For example:

At the end of the conflict a search was launched to locate every body.

Try those side dishes—every one is tasty!

here's/there's

'Here is' (or here's) is followed by a singular noun, and 'here are' by a plural noun. For example:

Here is your key *or* here are your keys
not here's your keys.

In the same way, 'there is' (or there's) is followed by a singular noun, and 'there are' by a plural noun. For example:

There is your paper *or* there are your papers
not there's your papers.

its

The pronoun 'its' is the possessive form of the singular 'it' (i.e. 'of it'). For example:

The book is praised for its design or the book's design is praised
not the book is praised for it's design.

majority/minority

With plural subjects, 'majority' and 'minority' take plural verbs. For example:

The majority of shareholders are overseas
not the majority of shareholders is overseas.

A minority of shareholders are here
not a minority of shareholders is here.

With singular subjects, 'majority' and 'minority' take singular verbs. For example:

The majority of the cake is eaten.
A minority of the party is still here.

Often using 'most' or 'few' is simpler. For example:

Most of the cake is eaten.
A few guests are still here.

measurement

Plural measurements, like other nouns, take plural verbs, but references to spans (e.g. time or distance) or quantities (e.g. weight or money) are in terms of single entities, and therefore take singular verbs. For example:

Two weeks have elapsed
but eight years is a long time to wait.

An amazing 280 kilograms of cocaine were seized
but 10 kilograms is a more typical haul.

none

This may take a singular or plural verb, depending on the context. If 'none' applies to individual members, a singular verb is appropriate. For example:

None of the plants is an orchid
not none of the plants are an orchid.

If 'none' applies to groups or several people, it takes a plural verb.

For example:

> I have many stones but none are precious
> *not* I have many stones but none is precious.

number

If 'number' is the main subject, it takes a singular verb. For example:

> The number of crimes is increasing
> *not* the number of crimes are increasing.

(Here, it is the total number, rather than the crimes, that is increasing.)

If 'number' is merely propping up the main subject, it takes a plural verb. For example:

> A large number of paintings are selling
> *not* a large number of paintings is selling.

(Here, it is the individual paintings, rather than the number, that are selling.)

their

The pronoun 'their' is the possessive form of the plural 'they' (i.e. 'of them'). For example:

> The children were praised for their awards
> *not* the children were praised for there awards
> *and not* the children were praised for they're awards.

If possible, resist using 'their' to refer to a singular subject as a strategy to avoid saying 'his or her'. Instead, try rephrasing the sentence using the plural. For example:

> Customers should be aware of their rights
> *not* the customer should be aware of their rights.

Note that 'theirs' does *not* take an apostrophe. For example:

> Did you know that the prizes are all theirs?
> *not* did you know that the prizes are all their's?

with/as well as

When these prepositions link a singular subject with another noun, they take a singular verb. For example:

> The auctioneer with his assistant is waiting
> *not* the auctioneer with his assistant are waiting.

> The olive oil as well as the garlic is ready
> *not* the olive oil as well as the garlic are ready.

The perils of possession

The word 'apostrophe' derives from the Greek *apostrephein*, meaning 'to turn away'. Growing out of a theatrical context, it gradually came to express more widely the idea of something missing, including a letter …

For a tiny symbol, the apostrophe causes great confusion. It is often omitted where needed, and inserted where it isn't needed or where it changes the intended meaning. Yet the rules governing possession are fairly simple. Where it is not used to indicate contraction (its original purpose), it indicates possession (i.e. belonging to). It should never be used to indicate a plural (e.g. cake's for sale!), a misuse popularly referred to as the 'greengrocer's apostrophe'.

Singular nouns

With most singular nouns and personal names, to indicate possession, add an apostrophe and 's'. For example:

> the mountain's peak (i.e. the peak of the mountain)
>
> Nadia's brother (i.e. the brother of Nadia)

This includes references to time. For example:

> one year's sabbatical (i.e. one year of sabbatical leave)

Singular nouns and personal names that end in 's' or 'ss' take an apostrophe and an additional 's'. For example:

> the cyclops's eye (i.e. the eye of the cyclops)
>
> the cross's centre (i.e. the centre of the cross)

Ros's arrival (i.e. the arrival of Ros)

Tess's departure (i.e. the departure of Tess)

Where nouns are jointly associated, the apostrophe is inserted after the second noun. For example:

her aunt and uncle's duplex
not her aunt's and uncle's duplex

In the absence of such association, the apostrophe is required after each noun. For example:

Federer's and Sampras's matches
not Federer and Sampras's matches

Note: The trend is, as ever, towards a simpler form of expression. The modern tendency of dropping the final 's' of names and allowing the apostrophe alone to indicate possession, although not universally condoned, has an obvious advantage with names that already end in 's', depending on the number of syllables. For example:

Mrs Bates's dress (i.e. one syllable, easy to pronounce)

Mr Connors's suit (i.e. two syllables, less pronounceable)

Yet opting to drop the final 's' in names of more than one syllable may lead to apparent inconsistency. For example:

Mrs Bates's dress and Mr Connors' suit

Unless referring to very many names in the possessive, therefore, it may be easiest to follow the conventional policy of simply adding an apostrophe and 's', regardless of the number of syllables in a name or its pronunciation.

That said, there are two main exceptions. First, the apostrophe is being formally dropped from names of places (unless it forms part of an actual name). For example:

Kings Cross, Earls Court *rather than* King's Cross, Earl's Court

Second, the second 's' is traditionally dropped from names of long-standing repute. For example:

> Moses' birth (i.e. the birth of Moses)
>
> Socrates' death (i.e. the death of Socrates)

Plural nouns

With plural nouns that end in 's', to indicate possession add an apostrophe alone. For example:

> the ladies' shower (i.e. the shower for ladies)
>
> the students' show (i.e. the show of the students)

Plural nouns that do not end in 's' take an apostrophe and 's'. For example:

> the children's recess (i.e. the recess for children)
>
> the men's sauna (i.e. the sauna for men)

This includes references to spans of time. For example:

> eight days' work (i.e. eight days of work, possessive)
> *but* the work will last eight days (descriptive)

Plural nouns that end in 'sses', though rare, take an apostrophe alone. For example:

> the crosses' position
> *not* the crosses's position

Such awkward plurals are best dealt with by rephrasing the sentence. For example:

> The position of the crosses is yet to be decided.

As with place names, the apostrophe is being dropped from names of institutions and other nouns (unless it forms part of an actual name) where the plural noun is descriptive or adjectival rather than possessive. For example:

Australian Book Publishers Association
not Australian Book Publishers' Association

a drivers licence
not a driver's licence

Pronouns

Possessive pronouns (i.e. 'my', 'mine', 'your', 'yours', 'his', 'hers', 'its', 'our', 'ours', 'their' and 'theirs') never take apostrophes. For example:

The car is hers and the house is theirs
not the car is her's and the house is their's.

Note, however, that as 'one' and 'body' take an apostrophe when possessive (i.e. one's, body's), so do compound pronouns containing '-one' and '-body'. For example:

someone's laughing, everybody's smiling
not someones laughing, everybodys smiling

its/it's

A common mistake is to insert an apostrophe into 'its' in an attempt to indicate possession—or as a grammatical safety net when we're unsure what to do. Remember, 'it's' is short for 'it is'; the apostrophe indicates a contraction, not possession. For example:

The dog wags its tail
not the dog wags it's tail.

its/their

Another error is to confuse 'its' (singular) with 'their' (plural). For example:

The restaurant has its own chef *or* restaurants have their own chefs
not the restaurant has their own chef.

Rather than using 'their' with a singular subject to avoid the 'his or her' sentence construction, try to rephrase the sentence using the plural. For example:

Artists should know their own materials
not an artist should know their own materials.

whose

'Whose' can apply both to people and things, and is both singular and plural. For example:

the surgeon whose latest operation is due

the castles whose walls are crumbling

The advantages of using 'whose' are clear when we compare

the castle whose wall is crumbling

with

the castle the wall of which is crumbling *or* the castle of which the wall is crumbling

Used interrogatively, however, 'whose' applies exclusively to people. For example:

Whose is this trumpet? (i.e. to whom does this trumpet belong?)

Note that 'whose' is *not* a contraction for 'who is' (i.e. who's). For example:

the builder who's working on site
not the builder whose working on site

Punctuation pitfalls

I was working on the proof of one of my poems all the morning, and took a comma out. In the afternoon I put it back again.

Attributed to Oscar Wilde, Irish dramatist and poet (1854–1900)

Here is an explanation of the main symbols of punctuation, with some typical errors.

Apostrophes

When it originally appeared in the sixteenth century, the apostrophe (') indicated a missing letter or letters.

The modern apostrophe is used in three ways.

Contraction

The most common use of the apostrophe is to denote a missing letter or letters. For example:

isn't *is short for* is not

should've *is short for* should have

Sixteenth-century literature, and Shakespeare's drama in particular, is rich in lyrical contractions that made some words easier for actors to pronounce. For example:

o'er *is short for* over

'tis *is short for* it is

Today, when an abbreviated word becomes fully anglicised, the apostrophe (or apostrophes) is dropped and the shortened form achieves the status of a word in its own right. For example:

All Hallows' Eve *became* Hallowe'en *and in turn* Halloween

forecastle *became* fo'c's'le *and in turn* focsle

Possession

The apostrophe is also used to indicate possession, where it means 'of' or 'belonging to'.

Most singular nouns take an apostrophe and 's'. For example:

the bat's wings (i.e. the wings of the bat)

the diver's splash (i.e. the splash of the diver)

Singular nouns that end in 's' or 'ss' take an apostrophe and an additional 's'. For example:

the atlas's cover (i.e. the cover of the atlas)

the dress's hem (i.e. the hem of the dress)

Plural nouns that do not end in 's' take an apostrophe and 's'. For example:

the men's group (i.e. the group of men)

the women's gowns (i.e. the gowns of the women)

Plural nouns that end in 's' or 'sses' take an apostrophe alone. For example:

the atlases' covers (i.e. the covers of the atlases)

the dresses' hems (i.e. the hems of the dresses)

Note: For a brief discussion on the modern practice of dropping the apostrophe with personal names and place names, see 'The perils of possession'.

Separation

The apostrophe is also used to separate plurals of single letters or numbers, for clarity. For example:

dot your i's and cross your t's

the high 2's

except with plurals of groups of letters or numbers. For example:

all the POWs

in the 1800s

unless the result would be unintelligible. For example:

do's and don'ts *is clearer than* dos and don'ts

if's and but's *is clearer than* ifs and buts

Brackets

There are two main types of brackets used in general writing: parentheses ( ) and square brackets [ ]. These are the brackets covered here.

Other brackets have specialised use: angle brackets < > are used to enclose web addresses, and curly brackets { } are used in mathematical contexts.

Parentheses

Colloquially referred to as 'round brackets', parentheses are used to partition off non-essential copy within a sentence. Such copy can consist of a single word, a phrase, or a sentence (and, rarely, several sentences). Sometimes pairs of commas or dashes can take the place of parentheses—the difference being that enclosing copy in parentheses emphasises its *non*-essentialness, whereas placing copy between commas or dashes includes the option of its being essential.

Typically, parentheses are used to add comments, explanations, definitions and examples as well as bibliographical references or references to figures, tables or other illustrative material. Relevant and interesting, they illuminate the text but are not crucial to an understanding of it. For example:

> If you see a good move on the chessboard, stop and look for a better one (paradoxical though it may sound, this principle will serve you well). (*comment*)
>
> A King is never actually taken (that is, putting your opponent's King in the position where capture is inevitable is the aim). (*explanation*)
>
> One way to protect your King and activate your Rook is to move the King two squares towards a Rook, then move that Rook onto the square crossed over by the King (known as 'castling'). (*definition*)
>
> Chess champions have suffered some memorable defeats by the computer (as illustrated by Kasparov's highly publicised defeat by Deep Blue in 1997). (*example*)
>
> José Raúl Capablanca, world chess champion 1921–7, photographed giving a simultaneous display (Edmonds & Eidinow 2004). (*bibliographical reference*)

Punctuating the text accompanying parentheses may cause confusion. If the enclosed text is a fragment of a complete sentence, place the final punctuation outside the closing parenthesis. For example:

> The 1972 Fischer–Spassky match at Reykjavik was hailed as 'the match of the century' (and 'the match of all time' according to the then President of the Icelandic Chess Federation).

If the enclosed text is a complete sentence, place the final punctuation (usually a full stop, but sometimes an exclamation mark or question mark) within the closing parenthesis. For example:

> The 1972 Fischer–Spassky match at Reykjavik was hailed as 'the match of the century'. (The then President of the Icelandic Chess Federation went further, calling it 'the match of all time'.)

Use parentheses sparingly, and keep enclosed copy as succinct as possible. Avoid using parentheses within parentheses as they cause needless confusion. Instead, repunctuate or rephrase the sentence. For example:

> The Reykjavik match or 'the match of all time' (as the then president of the Icelandic Chess Federation (Gudmundur Thórarinsson) described it in 1972) spectacularly ended the Soviet domination of the world of chess, catapulting chess into the realm of serious sport.

reads more clearly with a single set of parentheses:

> The Reykjavik match or 'the match of all time' (as the then president of the Icelandic Chess Federation, Gudmundur Thórarinsson, described it in 1972) spectacularly ended the Soviet domination of the world of chess, catapulting chess into the realm of serious sport

or with dashes:

> The Reykjavik match or 'the match of all time'—as the then president of the Icelandic Chess Federation, Gudmundur Thórarinsson, described it in 1972—spectacularly ended the Soviet domination of the world of chess, catapulting chess into the realm of serious sport.

Square brackets

Square brackets are used to signify interpolations in quotes in order to clarify a point, lend it emphasis, or indicate (by using the Latin *sic*, meaning 'thus') an error present in the original. For example:

> A sawyer will cut one hundred feet [30.5 metres] of timber for a bottle of spirits, value 2/6d [25 cents], which he drinks in a few hours. (*clarification*)
>
> William Bligh to Sir Joseph Banks, 7 February 1807, cited in HV Evatt, *Rum Rebellion*, Angus and Robertson, Sydney, 1965, p. 71

> Cook and Banks saw him [the Aboriginal] as he had ever been, in a state of balance with nature, not entirely freed from want … but able to survive *without extreme neurosis or fear* … [my italics]. (*emphasis*)
>
> A Moorhead, *The Fatal Impact*, Dell Publishing Co. Inc., New York, 1966, p. 127

> Tell Cormack McCaffery that this is a fine country and that I would recomend [*sic*] to him to come to this country as he would do well in it. (*indicating error in original*)
>
> Transcript of letter from Mr Montgomery, New South Wales, to his family in Ireland, 16 February 1840, Public Record Office of Northern Ireland, Crown Copyright 2007 (PRONI Reference: T3650/8)

The text accompanying square brackets is punctuated according to the same rules as text accompanying parentheses.

Colons

The colon (:) signals a relationship between the words on either side of it, with the first part leading to the second part. The colon separates less strongly than a semicolon, more than a comma, and is more formal than a dash. Like other punctuation that rounds off a sentence, it is followed by a single, not double, space.

The colon is used for various purposes.

For explanation

The colon is used to introduce a word or phrase that explains or expands on what precedes it. For example:

> The painting was the only mixed media on display: the artist had combined wax resins, raw pigments, fragments of disused mechanical objects, and acrylic paint dripped through patterned lace.

It can also be used to introduce a summary of what has gone before, or offer a comment on it. For example:

> The artist had combined wax resins, raw pigments, fragments of disused mechanical objects and acrylic paint dripped through patterned lace: the painting was truly mixed media.

For contrast

The colon is used to emphasise the second part of a sentence when it contrasts with, or is in opposition to, the first part (i.e. an antithesis). For example:

> He calls it abominable: I call it contemporary.

Introducing lists

The colon is usually placed after the lead-in sentence to introduce items in vertical lists. For example:

> The artist used:
>
> wax resins
> raw pigments
> mechanical fragments
> acrylic paint
> lace.

The colon also introduces items in horizontal lists when those items offer further information about something already referred to, or are preceded by 'as follows' or 'following'. For example:

> The artist's choice of materials was unusual: wax resins, raw pigments, fragments of disused mechanical objects and acrylic paint dripped through patterned lace.

> The artist's choice of materials was as follows: wax resins, raw pigments, fragments of disused mechanical objects and acrylic paint dripped through patterned lace.

Note that shorter lists of items that are integrated within the text as part of complete sentences do *not* require a colon. For example:

> The artist used wax resins, raw pigments, mechanical fragments and acrylic paint dripped through patterned lace.

Introducing quotations

The colon is used to introduce a quote that consists of a complete sentence and illustrates the preceding text. If brief, the quote may be integrated within the text. For example:

> Thatcher declared to widespread cheers: 'The lady's not for turning!'

If longer or emphatic, the quote may be displayed (referred to as a 'block quote'), indented and preceded by a line space. For example:

> In her speech to the Conservative Party Conference in 1980, Margaret Thatcher said:
>
> > To those waiting with bated breath for that favourite media catchphrase, the U-turn, I have only one thing to say. You turn if you want to. The lady's not for turning!

Note that incomplete quotes that are integrated within the text as part of complete sentences do *not* require a colon. For example:

> Thatcher's 'not for turning' speech stressed her resolve to stick to tough economic policies.

Introducing questions

The colon is used to introduce a question that is related to the preceding statement. The first word of a single question after a colon takes a lower-case letter, but the first words of multiple sentences take initial capital letters, unless incomplete. For example:

> The point is: why did you flee the country?
>
> The point is: why flee the country? or cover your traces? or lie to the family?
>
> The point is: Why did you flee the country? Why did you cover your traces? Why did you lie to the family?

Separating titles from subtitles

The colon is used to separate a title from its subtitle. Note that the word after a colon does *not* require a capital letter unless initial capitals are used for all the main words in that subtitle. For example:

> 'Actorphobia: the five-day cure' (*article*)
>
> 'Japan's Yasukuni shrine: place of peace or conflict?' (*dissertation*)
>
> *Kiri: Her Unsung Story* (*book*)
>
> *Law & Order: Criminal Intent* (*TV program*)

In dialogues and transcripts

The colon is used after speakers' names in dialogues. For example:

> *Vladimir:* That passed the time.
>
> *Estragon:* It would have passed in any case.
>
> *Vladimir:* Yes, but not so rapidly.
>
> S Beckett, *Waiting for Godot*, Act I

The colon is also used in this way in transcripts, from formal interviews to conversations. For example:

> REPORTER: Are you saying that you were forced to work for this factory?
>
> ANTONIONI: More than that, I was forced to ...
>
> REPORTER: What were you forced to do, Mr Antonioni?
>
> ANTONIONI: I was forced to lie for them. Yeah, absolutely.

Expressing ratios

The colon is used mathematically to express ratios, whether displayed or as part of a sentence. Used like this, there is no space either side of the colon. For example:

> cement, sand and crushed stone mixed in a ratio of 1:2:5
>
> the male:female ratio

Note that British English uses full stops in expressions of time to separate hours and minutes (e.g. 10.45 am), whereas American English uses colons (e.g. 10:45 am).

Commas

Of all the punctuation marks, the comma (,) is the most frequently used. Organised religion was instrumental in formulating punctuation rules to prevent the misreading of sacred texts, but it wasn't until the invention of the printing press in 1439 that commas, like other punctuation marks, became standardised.

Today, as then, the comma is used to indicate a pause at a place where we would naturally take a breath. Commas function as an aid to understanding; by breaking up a sentence into smaller portions, they help us to grasp its meaning more quickly. We are more sparing in our use of commas now than in past centuries, and many writers prefer not to use them unless they are absolutely necessary (Peter Carey's *True History of the Kelly Gang* notably uses no commas at all). Beyond that, how we use commas is largely a matter of personal choice as well as of nuance and emphasis.

The indispensable comma

The one comma whose existence is not debatable is that which is essential for clarity and if omitted, or positioned wrongly, can alter a meaning. For example:

> Many years before, he had met the twins while travelling in India ...

has a quite different meaning when the comma is removed:

> Many years before he had met the twins while travelling in India ...

which appears to refer to a time *before* 'he' had ever met the twins, whereas in fact the writer is referring to a time many years ago *when* 'he' had met the twins. In addition, the lack of a comma results in ambiguity as to who was doing the travelling.

An additional comma before the last item in a list may likewise be essential to prevent ambiguity. For example:

> The committee was attended by the Director, the Head of Technology and Infrastructure, and Corporate Services personnel

becomes confusing if the second comma is left out:

> The committee was attended by the Director, the Head of Technology and Infrastructure and Corporate Services personnel

because it is not clear whether 'Infrastructure' belongs with the Head of Technology or with Corporate Services personnel.

A comma may be required to separate two identical words. For example:

> Once she had seen it, it no longer scared her.

A comma may also be desirable when a sentence contains numerals. For example:

> In 1347, 800 people a day died from the Black Death in some European cities

has an obvious advantage over

> In 1347 800 people a day died from the Black Death in some European cities.

If the numeral itself contains a comma, the potential for confusion increases and it is safer to rephrase the sentence. For example:

> In August 1945, the atom bombs dropped in Japan killed 200,000 people

is clearer than

> In August 1945, 200,000 people died from the atom bombs dropped in Japan.

After an introduction

One of the simplest uses of the comma is after an introductory word or phrase at the beginning of a sentence. For example:

> Well, he could never have done it without your help.
>
> As we all know, a life in politics is not for the faint-hearted.

Breaking up long sentences

Most commonly of all, the comma is used to break up a longer sentence into more manageable clauses, each with their own subject. For example:

> When a violent explosion tore through the fragile skin of the Apollo 13 spacecraft in April 1970, NASA mounted the most dramatic rescue mission in the history of human exploration.

In particular, the comma is often used before 'and', 'but' and 'or'. For example:

> The ancient Mayans developed the use of the zero, and it was this that helped them devise a highly sophisticated calendar by 360 BC.

Pairs of commas

Commas are used parenthetically to break up non-restrictive, or commenting, clauses (i.e. clauses that provide non-essential information). For example:

> Students who study scriptwriting, especially those doing the serial writing courses, have to adhere to realistic deadlines.

A common error is using only one comma where a pair is needed, in much the same way as using only one of a pair of brackets. If the writer of the previous sentence, for example, were guilty of this it would read:

> Students who study scriptwriting, especially those doing the serial writing courses have to adhere to realistic deadlines
>
> *or*
>
> Students who study scriptwriting especially those doing the serial writing courses, have to adhere to realistic deadlines

both of which are, at best, perplexing.

For emphasis

Commas are used, often in pairs, for emphasis. This can take the form of ironic detachment on the part of the writer from the sentiment expressed. For example:

> Mr Julius, apparently, believed that she would always come back to him.

The commas enclosing 'apparently' inject an element of disbelief—even, depending on what we know of the speaker, scorn or amusement—that Mr Julius should persist in believing that 'she' would return. Without the commas the effect is altered:

> Mr Julius apparently believed that she would always come back to him

is a straightforward statement of fact, connotation-free, describing Mr Julius' belief that 'she' would return.

In lists

Multiple commas are used to separate names or items listed in a sentence, although not before the final 'and' or 'or'. For example:

> Sarah was accompanied by Thomas, Veronica and Lucas.
>
> The sailors survived on a diet of cod, pork, peas and biscuits.

If more detailed information accompanies the names or items, an additional comma is placed before the last item. For example:

> Sarah was accompanied by an angry Thomas, a particularly naughty Veronica, and an uncharacteristically subdued Lucas.

> The sailors on sixteenth-century European voyages survived on a diet of dried cod, salt pork, dried peas, and weevil-ridden ships' biscuits.

When *not* to use commas

Commas are not necessary in restrictive, or defining, clauses (i.e. clauses that provide essential information). For example:

> Anyone who can't stand the sight of blood, should not enter medical school

reads more smoothly without the comma:

> Anyone who can't stand the sight of blood should not enter medical school.

Nor should commas be used as a linking device between independent clauses. For example:

> The company made 21 appointments during the year, eight were women

should either be rewritten:

> The company made 21 appointments, of which eight were women
> (*or* eight of which were women)

or split into two separate sentences and punctuated accordingly:

> The company made 21 appointments; eight were women.

Extremely brief sentences do not normally need commas. For example:

> With you here, she feels safe

reads more fluidly without a pause:

> With you here she feels safe.

The commas that traditionally followed all adjectives but the last in a series preceding a noun are now, by general consensus, usually dropped. For example:

> the expensive, brown, suede shoes

tends to be written comma-less:

> the expensive brown suede shoes

Although neither is incorrect, separating adjectives with commas still serves a purpose in stressing every adjective, making each more emphatic.

Dashes

> There are three types of dash: the en rule (–), the em rule (—), and the 2-em rule (——).

The en rule

The en rule, longer than a hyphen but shorter than a dash, is a linking device based on the width of a lower-case 'n' (or half the width of the em rule).

It is used in two ways.

First, the en rule is used to indicate a range of numerals or span of time. For example:

pp 29–31	$15–20	12–15 apples
2.30–3.45 pm	July–August 2017	1798–1945

Note that it is *not* appropriate to use the en rule with the phrases 'between — and —' or 'from — to —'. For example:

> between 1939 and 1945 *not* between 1939–1945
>
> from 1939 to 1945 *not* from 1939–1945

Second, the en rule links people or things, indicating a relationship between them. For example:

a father–daughter relationship	an import–export business
the blue–green sea	the Turkish–Syrian border

There must be an equivalence between what is being linked. For example:

the blue–green sea
not a bluish–green sea
and not a blue–greenish sea

the Turkish–Syrian border
not the Turkish–Syria border
and not the Turkey–Syrian border

The en rule is unspaced, unless one of the words being linked itself consists of two or more words, in which case it is spaced. For example:

an All Blacks – Springboks final

the Las Vegas – Los Angeles flight

In mathematical contexts, when used to indicate a minus sign the en rule is spaced, unless it represents a negative number. For example:

100 – 80 = 20   –18 °C

The em rule

The em rule is the most common of all dashes and is broadly referred to as 'the dash'. Stronger than a comma yet less formal than the colon or parentheses, the em rule, unlike the en rule, is a separating device. It is based on the width of a capital 'M'. Note that British English tends to use a spaced en rule, whereas American English uses an unspaced em rule. The em rule should be used sparingly and not combined with a colon (i.e. :—).

The em rule is used in three ways.

First, the em rule indicates a sudden change, where a sentence is either interrupted completely or resumes in a different, often unexpected, direction. For this reason it appears frequently in dialogue. For example:

> 'We had just reached the castle door—.' Her voice faltered, and she burst into tears.

> 'We had just reached the castle door when—oh, I'll tell you about that later.'

It is also used more loosely to separate segments of a sentence. For example:

> He bolted from the castle as fast as he could—once his friends were safe.

Avoid this use of the em rule in formal writing. If a comma or different punctuation mark causes a loss of emphasis, try rephrasing the sentence. For example:

> Once his friends were safe, he bolted from the castle as fast as he could.

Second, the em rule indicates a break in the sentence to introduce an explanation or amplification. For example:

> We're meant to be a little baffled too—tantalised by hints and echoes.

> The engine made a noise—a harsh grinding sound that grew louder by the minute.

It is also used to introduce a humorous contrast to what has gone before, or a paraphrase or summary of it. For example:

> I can't tell her that I grew up on the streets—imagine what her family would say!

> The post was senior, the perks excellent and the timing ideal—in short, it was a great job.

Third, the em rule is used parenthetically, like a pair of brackets, to enclose one or two words, a brief phrase, or a longer statement. For example:

> He couldn't—or wouldn't?—answer.
>
> 'As a matter of fact'—she paused for thought—'I don't remember seeing anyone either leave or enter the ice rink on Saturday morning.'
>
> For an opera of such logistical complexity—the score requires an orchestra of over one hundred players, some seventy percussion instruments, a jazz combo and various electronics—it has been staged remarkably often.

Thus enclosed, briefer statements tend to be more effective than very long or discursive ones which can be hard to follow. For this reason, approach a parenthetical use of em rules with discretion. Do not use more than one pair of em rules in a sentence, or more than one pair in a paragraph.

The 2-em rule

The 2-em rule, unlike both the en rule and the em rule, indicates omission. As its name suggests, it consists of two em rules placed side by side.

The 2-em rule is used in three ways.

First, it is used to indicate the omission of sensitive names. For example:

> J—— received maximum protection under the witness protection program.

Second, the 2-em rule is used in bibliographical or reference lists to indicate one or more works by the preceding author and thus avoid repetition. For example:

> TP Wiseman, *Catullus and his World: A Reappraisal*, Cambridge University Press, 1985.

——*The Roman Audience: Classical Literature as Social History*, Oxford University Press, 2015.

Third, the 2-em rule is used within text, usually speech, to avoid profanity, although this usage is declining. The initial letter of an expression may or may not be included. For example:

'Don't be so —— mean!'

'Don't be so f—— mean!'

The 2-em rule is spaced unless the word it is replacing retains an initial letter or letters, in which case it is unspaced, as in the example above.

Ellipses

The ellipsis (…) consists of three full stops with a space before and afterwards. When it appears at the end of a sentence, it does not need a full stop.

The ellipsis is used in two ways.

Omission

The ellipsis is used to indicate the intentional omission of an essential word or words from a quote (from the Greek *élleipsis*, meaning 'omission'). For example:

'The inflation rate is … driven by increasing numbers of foreign businesses pulling out and the collapse in the black market value of the Zimbabwean dollar,' a respected source in Harare said yesterday.

'The inflation rate is largely driven by increasing numbers of foreign businesses pulling out and the collapse … of the Zimbabwean dollar,' a respected source in Harare said yesterday.

Note that an inappropriately placed ellipsis can alter the meaning of a sentence. For example:

> 'The inflation rate is largely driven by … the collapse in the black market value of the Zimbabwean dollar,' a respected source in Harare said yesterday

implies, erroneously, that the 'respected source' is suggesting that the collapse in the Zimbabwean dollar is the main factor influencing Zimbabwe's rising inflation rate.

Note also that if an entire paragraph is being omitted, the ellipsis is placed on a line by itself.

Vagueness or incompletion

The ellipsis is used more generally to indicate vague, meandering or incomplete thoughts, including those that drift off into silence. This is particularly common in fiction when the writer is trying to capture or mimic a character's manner of thinking or speaking. For example:

> She'd been so young, hardly more than a baby …

> I wish … Um … ah … there must be a reason for all this …

Beware of overusing ellipses to increase a sense of excitement or mystery. When this happens, ellipses become an excuse for lazy writing and their effect wears thin. For instance, the first statement above is effective, but the second—depending on the speech patterns of the speaker—can be tightened up without any loss of atmosphere.

For example:

> I wish—I don't know! There must be a reason for all this …

Sometimes a statement can be rounded off and an ellipsis left out altogether:

> I wish—oh, I don't know! There must be a reason for all this, but what can it be?

Exclamation marks

The exclamation mark (!) is used after exclamations for emphasis, and is one of the most popular symbols of punctuation.

The exclamation mark is used in two ways.

Emphasising emotions

The exclamation mark is used to emphasise strong or exaggerated emotions. It can convey a range of feelings, from surprise, delight or approval to regret, indignation or sarcasm—and sometimes sheer volume. For this reason, it is often used in fiction and informal writing. For example:

> Who would've thought you'd end up on the stage! (*surprise*)
>
> How we loved that play! (*delight*)
>
> What amazing stage lighting! (*approval*)
>
> If only I'd locked my front door! (*regret*)
>
> Any half-efficient porter would've spotted an intruder! (*indignation*)
>
> So you finally called the police—that's just great! (*sarcasm*)
>
> I am absolutely furious! (*volume*)

Warnings and commands

The exclamation mark is used with warnings and commands, including single-word interjections, as well with rhetorical questions and some greetings. For example:

> Railings faulty—do not touch! (*warning*)
>
> Attention, please! (*command*)
>
> Oh! Is that him? Help! (*interjection*)
>
> How dare she say that! (*rhetorical question*)
>
> Welcome, ladies and gentlemen! (*greeting*)

Of all the symbols of punctuation, the exclamation mark is the most overused and overburdened. As its name implies, it is intended to accompany exclamations, not straightforward statements. An exclamation mark does little to spice up a tired sentence, and a passage sprinkled with them quickly becomes irritating. To add drama or humour, alter the words or the way in which they are used. For example:

> This is a disgrace!

should more properly read

> What a disgrace! (*exclamation*)
>
> *or*
>
> This is a disgrace. (*statement*)

In general writing, particularly fiction, use the exclamation mark sparingly, and in formal and academic writing it is generally best avoided altogether.

When *not* to use exclamation marks

Resist doubling or trebling exclamation marks for greater effect, or using a whole string of them. For example:

> The stock market's crashed!!!

is no clearer than

> The stock market's crashed!

Rephrasing a statement is one way to make it more emphatic. For example:

> Guess what—the stock market's crashed!

Using italics also indicates emphasis. For example:

> Guess what—the stock market's *crashed*!

Do not combine exclamation marks with other punctuation, in particular question marks, to strengthen their effect. For example:

> Why is the premium so high?!

is no more emphatic than

> Why is the premium so high?

The raising of the question itself carries with it an implicit scepticism as to the level of premium; an exclamation mark is superfluous. Again, rephrasing or italicising can help make the question more emphatic. For example:

> Why on earth is the premium so high?
>
> *or*
>
> Why is the premium so *high*?

Finally, there is no need to add full stops after exclamation marks. For example:

> What an exorbitant charge!.

should read

> What an exorbitant charge!

Full stops

The full stop (.), also known as the 'full point' or 'period', is most commonly used to indicate the end of a sentence. It is followed by a single space.

The full stop is used in five ways.

Full statements and fragments of statements

The full stop is used to indicate the end of a complete sentence that is a statement or, more colloquially, a fragment of a statement. For example:

> I want to learn to sail a boat. (*full statement*)
>
> When would I find time to sail? On weekends. (*fragment of statement*)

Clear and unambiguous? Perhaps not. Many times we come across distinct statements being forced into too close a relationship by 'and' rather than given separate identity by a full stop. For example:

> By the end of the course you will be confident sailing under reasonable weather conditions, you will also have gained an understanding of knots, rules of the road, and wind direction.

This is a clear case of lack of sequence, and should read:

> By the end of the course you will be confident sailing under reasonable weather conditions. You will also have gained an understanding of knots, rules of the road, and wind direction.

Unlike most other punctuation marks, the full stop is frequently under-used. Don't overlook the one big advantage of a short sentence: clarity!

Indirect questions

The full stop is used after an indirect question. For example:

> She enquired where the nearest sailing school was.
>
> They asked her why she wanted to know.

Formal instructions

The full stop is used after a formal instruction. For example:

> Please dress simply and leave all jewellery at home when stepping aboard.
>
> Would everyone please raise a glass to the captain.

Abbreviations

The 'full stop' (as it is called in British English) or 'period' (as it is called in American English) is used after abbreviations (i.e. shortened forms of words where the last letter is changed). For example:

Co. (Company) tel. (telephone) vol. (volume)

The full stop is also used in Latin abbreviations. For example:

c. (*circa*, meaning 'around' or 'about')

etc. (*et cetera*, meaning 'and so on')

except when those abbreviations are fully anglicised. For example:

e.g. (*exempli gratia*, meaning 'for example')

i.e. (*id est*, meaning 'that is')

The full stop has also been dropped from symbols of measurement. For example:

cm kg mL

British English does *not* use full stops in contractions (i.e. abbreviations that retain their first and last letters), acronyms (i.e. abbreviations made up from initial letters or syllables that are pronounced as words), and initialisms (abbreviations made up from initial letters that are pronounced as such). This applies to both capitals and lower-case letters. For example:

Dr	Mrs	St	(*contractions*)
Anzac	AWOL	NATO	(*acronyms*)
EU	IRA	UK	(*initialisms*)

Nor are full stops used in people's initials or academic or professional qualifications. For example:

AL Cruz MB BS FRACGP FAMA

JR Quinn BA MA GradDipLib PhD

Note that there is a greater acceptance of the use of full stops in American English, particularly in certain contractions and initialisms. For example:

Dr.	Mr.	St. Louis	(*contractions*)
U.S.A.	U.S.S.R.	Washington D.C.	(*initialisms*)

Mathematical contexts

Full stops are used in money and numbers (as decimal points) as well as in time (to separate hours and minutes). For example:

$24.99 3.5% 4.55 am

When *not* to use full stops

Full stops are not needed after sentences that end with exclamation marks, question marks and ellipses. For example:

Always make sure you carry life jackets!

Did you give way to vessels under oars?

Sailing at sunset is so romantic …

Full stops are also not needed after headings, including those that are long and complex. For example:

Reef knots (*simple heading*)

Ropes and cordage: Synthetic versus natural materials (*longer heading*)

Nor are full stops needed after captions, including those that are complete sentences, unless captions consist of two or more sentences that function as mini-paragraphs. For example:

Tacking hard to windward (*simple caption, incomplete sentence*)

Reaching is the fastest sailing position (*simple caption, complete sentence*)

> Gradually disappearing from the yachting scene, schooner rigs remain the most graceful of all rigs. They carry two masts, and typically more than one headsail. The divided rig illustrated above carries two sails between the masts. (*longer caption, several sentences*)

Finally, full stops are not needed after labels in diagrams, pictures and tables. Typically these consist of one or two words or a brief sentence. For example:

> Anti-snarl gear
>
> Gybing the spinnaker
>
> Large spinnakers can quickly get out of hand

Hyphens

Shorter than both the dash and the en rule, the hyphen (-) is essentially a linking device for bringing together words or parts of words.

The hyphen is used in three ways.

Creating compound words

The hyphen is used to link words that have a relationship to each other, to form a single expression. For example:

cat-o'-nine-tails	cul-de-sac	go-between
south-east	three-quarters	two-up

The use of the hyphen in compound words consisting of two nouns is gradually disappearing. The trend is for such words to appear first separately, then to become hyphenated, and finally to combine as a single new word. If in doubt, check in the dictionary before assuming that a hyphen is necessary. For example:

> tool shed → tool-shed → toolshed
>
> were wolf → were-wolf → werewolf

Linking words adjectivally

The hyphen is used to link together two or more words to make an adjective (i.e. they are used attributively, before a noun). For example:

> the advertisement-free magazine
>
> the company-funded projects

In this context, a hyphen may be necessary to prevent ambiguity. For example:

> the advertisement-free magazine (i.e. refers to a magazine that is free of advertisements *not* to a free magazine)
>
> the company-funded projects (i.e. refers specifically to those projects that are funded by the company *not* to the fact that the company funded certain projects)

When a meaning is unambiguous, such as with adverbs ending in '-ly', a hyphen is not needed. For example:

> the carefully executed plan (i.e. can only mean 'the plan that is executed carefully')
>
> the roughly mannered man (i.e. can only mean 'the man whose manners are rough')

Also, when words are not linked adjectivally no hyphen is needed. For example:

> a well-known carpenter *but* the carpenter is well known
>
> the world-renowned surgeon *but* the surgeon is world renowned

In prefixes

The hyphen is used in some words containing prefixes, but not all. Everyday prefixes include:

> anti-, auto-, co-, counter-, de-, ex-, extra-, inter-, neo-, non-, post-, pre-, pro-, re-, semi-, un-

We regularly encounter, for example:

> anti-war, auto-ignition, co-workers, counter-terrorism, de-skill, ex-wife, extra-special, inter-school, neo-colonial, non-fat, post-production, pre-exist, pro-life, re-educate, semi-industrial, un-American

but also

> antisocial, automatic, coordinate, counteract, deconstruct, exchange, extraordinary, international, neonatal, nonsense, postcard, preoccupy, proactive, reassure, semifinal, unemployed

How, then, do we know when to use a hyphen with a prefix? British English hyphenates to a greater extent than does American English, which more readily accepts compound words. As there is no absolute rule determining whether words with prefixes take hyphens or not, it makes sense to base your decisions on clarity. In other words, if a hyphen is necessary to avoid ambiguity, or assists clarity, use one; if not, don't.

There are three situations where a hyphen is obligatory, or highly desirable.

First, when a hyphen is necessary to prevent misreading of a word or sentence, and its absence would alter the intended meaning. For example:

> co-op (i.e. a cooperative organisation)
> coop (i.e. an enclosure for poultry)

> re-count (i.e. to count again)
> recount (i.e. to narrate)

Second, when a hyphen prevents confusion by separating identical or similar-sounding vowels. For example:

> auto-immune *is clearer than* autoimmune

> pre-empt *is clearer than* preempt

Third, when a hyphen prevents a word from becoming excessively long. For example:

inter-denominational *is clearer than* interdenominational

ultra-orthodox *is clearer than* ultraorthodox

Breaking words at line ends

The hyphen is used to indicate where a word has been broken off at the end of a line and carried over to the next. British English tends to break words according to derivation (e.g. aristo-cracy), whereas American English breaks words according to pronunciation (e.g. aristoc-racy). That aside, there are universal rules to be observed when deciding where to break a word:

- Avoid breaking words of less than six letters and proper names.
- Avoid breaking syllables, or clusters of letters that make a single sound (e.g. invest-ment, king-dom).
- Avoid breaking words of one syllable, regardless of how many letters they have (e.g. queue, scythe).
- Most words can be broken between two consonants, identical or not (e.g. clap-ping, prob-lem).
- Words that are formed with prefixes or suffixes should be broken at that point even if they consist of two letters (e.g. un-kind, wild-ly).
- With all other words, keep a minimum of three letters on a line (e.g. gov-ern-ment, rel-eg-ate).
- Keep numerals and units of measurements together (e.g. 2.5 cm *not* 2.5-cm).
- If a word is already hyphenated, break it at its existing hyphen rather than hyphenating it again (e.g. spring-clean, witch-hunt).

- Avoid 'suspended' or 'hanging' hyphens (e.g. 'Do you work full- or part-time?' can be rephrased 'Do you work full-time or part-time?').
- Avoid hyphenating strings of words (e.g. '... and you-all-know-who-I-mean ...').
- Avoid two or more consecutive lines ending with hyphens by rephrasing the sentence or respacing the line.

Question marks

The question mark or interrogation point (?) is placed at the end of a sentence or fragment of a sentence to indicate a query. The term 'question mark' was coined in the late 1800s. Among the various theories as to its origin, the most likely is that it derives from the Latin *quaestio*, meaning 'question', and abbreviated with a capital 'Q' placed over a lower-case 'o', which in time took the form we use today.

The question mark is used in three ways.

Direct questions

The question mark turns a complete sentence, part of a sentence, or a single word into a direct question. For example:

> When did the volcano last erupt?
>
> It last erupted when?
>
> Really?

This includes rhetorical questions, to which no answer is expected. For example:

> Who could fail to be impressed by the casts of the victims fleeing Pompeii?

If necessary, the question mark can be placed mid-sentence. For example:

> Who could fail to be impressed? she wondered.

Note that reported questions (i.e. indirect questions), being statements, do *not* need question marks. For example:

> I asked if the volcano last erupted in 1944.
>
> *or*
>
> I asked: 'Did the volcano last erupt in 1944?'
>
> *not*
>
> I asked if the volcano had last erupted in 1944?

Note also that statements phrased as direct questions that function as formal or polite instructions do *not* need question marks. For example:

> Would visitors please keep to the designated walkway.

Implied questions

The question mark is also used with implied questions. It has a powerful role here, turning what would otherwise be a statement into a question. For example:

> This volcano is still considered active?
>
> These frescoes date from 64 BC?

Expressing uncertainty

The question mark is also used before a word or number that is difficult to verify, or over which there is debate. This occurs predominantly in historical accounts, where it often appears within parentheses. For example:

> The inscription indicates that the young Marcus died from inhalation of poisonous sulphuric gases at (?) Stabiae.
>
> Pliny the Younger (?61–112 BC), lawyer, writer and philosopher, wrote a famously detailed and vivid eye-witness account of the eruption of Mt Vesuvius.

Do not use multiple question marks in an effort to achieve greater effect. For example:

> If the eruption is meant to have occurred on 24 August (summer), why were the wine fermenting jars already sealed over, which would have happened in late October???

Raising the question of the apparent discrepancy between the universally accepted date of the eruption of Mt Vesuvius and this detail of the wine-making customs of its people is achieved with a single question mark. The two additional question marks do not make the question more valid, and serve only to distract.

Quotation marks

Quotation marks ('quote marks' for short) or speech marks (") signal speech that is directly quoted. Use the 'curved' quotes (also known as 'six and nine' quotes, 'book quotes', or to use Microsoft Word-speak, 'smart' quotes) rather than the older style, straight quotes that are a leftover from the days of the typewriter.

British English tends to favour single quote marks, and double quotes to indicate quotes within quotes. For example:

> 'It has integrity,' she said.
>
> 'They told me to use the word "integrity" in the advertisement,' she said.

American English adheres more consistently to double quote marks, with single ones reserved for quotes within quotes. For example:

> "It has integrity," she said.
>
> "They told me to use the word 'integrity' in the advertisement," she said.

In practice, many publishing houses and organisations adopt the policy they feel suits them best. The following examples use single quote marks. Whichever policy you use, be consistent.

Quote marks are used in four ways.

Quotations

Quote marks are used around words that are directly quoted from another source. For example:

> 'The play is a masterpiece of understatement,' the review stated. 'The dialogue, finely calibrated to expose the tension between the characters, reminds us that words can be a weapon as much as a tool for communication.'

With longer quotes that run to several paragraphs (called 'block quotes'), opening quote marks are placed at the start of each paragraph, but closing quote marks are only placed at the close of the last paragraph.

Direct and reported speech

Quote marks are used around all speech (with the exception of transcripts of plays and other documents where people's names precede their speech). Monologues and very brief exchanges may be incorporated into the surrounding text. For example:

> 'I was fascinated with the theatre as a child,' he said. 'I saw my first stage play at nine and never forgot it.'

To capture extended conversations, use a new line for each new speaker. For example:

> 'I don't want to go,' she said.
>
> 'Not even if I ask you?' he leaned forwards.
>
> '*Especially* if you ask me,' she replied.

The punctuation of quotes can be confusing. British English retains that if the punctuation is part of the quote, the punctuation is placed within the quote marks; if the punctuation is not part of the quote, it is placed outside the quote marks. For example:

> 'I was an outcast. I felt as if I were standing by a window and could see life going on near me but could never be part of it.'
>
> He described himself as an 'outcast'.

Subject matter also plays a role in the treatment of punctuation in quotes in British English. In modern fiction, punctuation is usually placed within the quotes; in nonfiction and business documents, the placement of punctuation is often dictated by house style, and so varies from publisher to publisher.

The American convention is simpler, if a shade less logical. In all subject matter, American English consistently places the punctuation inside the (double) quote marks regardless of whether the punctuation is part of the quote or not, and regardless of the length of the quote (including one consisting of a single word). For example:

> "I was an outcast. I felt as if I were standing by a window and could see life going on near me but could never be part of it."
>
> He described himself as an "outcast."

For emphasis

Quote marks are used to draw attention to an unusual word or phrase, or a word or phrase used in an unusual way. For example:

> From the earliest age, my parents instilled in me the need to 'live up to my potential'. It became a sort of mantra in my house. What they meant by 'potential' I never quite knew ...

Italics also serve to emphasise an expression, although in a more general sense. Enclosing an expression in quote marks suggests that it has acquired a specific meaning or association—in this case, 'potential' became synonymous with parental pressure, a rainbow-like thing which the child could never attain.

Quote marks can also be used to inflect a word or phrase with irony (which is why they are also known as 'scare quotes'). For example:

> Sarah said that her brother claimed to have 'great respect' for mainstream art, that of course it had nothing to do with the benefits he reaped from it.

The use of quote marks around 'great respect' tells us that Sarah sees more than an element of hypocrisy in her brother's embracing of mainstream art.

Be careful not to overuse quote marks for emphasis, which diminishes their impact and appears pretentious. In particular, avoid using them with well-known or humorous expressions, and with slang or nicknames.

Quote marks can be used to introduce technical terms or terms with specialised meanings, usually followed by a definition. For example:

> In this context, 'black box' refers to a sort of flexible studio theatre where actors and audience share the room, surrounded by black tabs, or curtains.

Indicating titles of short works

Despite the inevitable variations between established styles, quote marks are usually used to refer to segments of works such as chapters within books, short stories, essays, articles in magazines or journals, articles in newspapers, episodes within radio or television programs, and unpublished documents. For example:

> 'Knots and splices' (*chapter*)
>
> 'Bernice bobs her hair' (*short story*)
>
> 'The function of criticism' (*essay*)
>
> 'Lose weight and feel fabulous!' (*magazine article*)
>
> 'Tourist hotspots hit by noxious slick' (*newspaper article*)
>
> 'Down in the basement' (*radio program*)
>
> 'Wirrangul women: Always have, always will' (*television program*)
>
> 'Microbial diseases of corals and global warming' (*unpublished document*)

Quote marks are also used for titles of songs or short poems (titles of long poems are treated as book titles, and italicised). For example:

'Smoke gets in your eyes' (*song*)

'Whispers of immortality' (*short poem*)

Semicolons

The semicolon (;) signals a break that is more definite than a comma but less definite than a full stop. It is one of the more under-used, and misused, symbols of punctuation, yet the rules governing it are straightforward and, in moderation, it can tighten up writing and lend it rhythm.

The semicolon is used in two ways.

Linking clauses

The semicolon is used to link two independent but related clauses. Often these two clauses work together towards a similarity of thought or feeling; they balance each other and are complementary. For example:

> The air grew heavy as the crowd surged forwards; I knew that I was about to faint.

The gentle joining of two clauses can be more appropriate than using a full stop to separate them entirely, which can lead to an overly abrupt break and two very short sentences. For example:

> The air grew heavy as the crowd surged forwards. I knew that I was about to faint.

On the other hand, using a conjunction (e.g. 'and' or 'but') to create a single, longer sentence may also prove unsatisfactory. For example:

> The air grew heavy as the crowd surged forwards, and I knew that I was about to faint.

Although the sentence is grammatically faultless, the lack of emphasis and rhythm detracts from its impact.

The semicolon can also be used to juxtapose two clauses where there is a contrast of thought or feeling. In the absence of a conjunction after the semicolon, the second clause is often introduced by words such as 'however', 'therefore' or 'nevertheless'. For example:

> The air grew heavy as the crowd surged forwards; nevertheless, I felt confident that this time I would not faint.

Again, the contrast between the menacing situation and confidence of the writer to remain resilient is more effective than if the statement were split into two sentences or presented as a single, longer one joined by a conjunction.

Separating items in lists

The semicolon is also used to separate a list of items in which commas are already used. For example:

> To celebrate the opening of our cellars we are offering a 35% discount on our Rosé, with vibrant blackberry flavours; our Verdelho, with lifted aromas of pineapple, guava and honeysuckle; and our Shiraz, with rich cherry flavours and hints of chocolate and pepper.

Such lists are often preceded by an introductory sentence and a colon. For example:

> To celebrate the opening of our new cellars we are offering a 35% discount on three cases: our Rosé, with vibrant blackberry flavours; our Verdelho, with lifted aromas of pineapple, guava and honeysuckle; and our Shiraz, with rich cherry flavours and hints of chocolate and pepper.

The practice of using a semicolon at the end of each item in vertical bulleted lists has been largely discarded. In summary, if items consist of incomplete sentences, use lower-case letters and no punctuation except a full stop after the final item; if items consist of complete sentences, use capital letters and full stops after each one.

Note: For details on punctuating lists, see 'Lists'.

Separating bibliographical details

The semicolon is used to separate bibliographical details listed together within in-text citations, so that the end of one reference is clearly distinguished from the beginning of the next.

This applies to multiple works by the same author or co-authors as well as various works by multiple authors. For example:

> Goldstein, Murray and Grant (2014, p. 67; 2001, p. 98; 1999, pp. 104) argue that ...
>
> ... proposed the theory (Cottrell 2007, p. 4; Fischer 2002, p. 22; Frazer 1999, p. 72).

Slashes

The slash (/), also known as the 'oblique', 'stroke' or 'solidus', is one of the lesser-used symbols of punctuation.

The slash is used in four ways.

Alternatives

The slash is used to separate alternatives. It is therefore common in official forms such as applications and surveys. For example:

> please circle: yes/no
>
> the wine and/or cheese platter
>
> would he/she (or s/he) please contact reception

Abbreviations

The slash is used as an abbreviation of 'a', 'an' or 'per' in units of measurement. For example:

a speed limit of 80 km/hr

petrol at $1.20/litre

soil density of 1.25g/cm^3

Note that the slash should *not* be used with units of measurements that are spelled out. For example:

2 km/hr *or* two kilometres an hour
not two kilometres/hour

The slash is also used within some more general abbreviations. For example:

a/c (*account*) E.g. Credit, cheque or savings a/c?

c/ (*care of*) E.g. Write to me c/82 Waimanu Road, Suva, Fiji.

n/a (*not applicable* or *not available*) E.g. Results of exam n/a

Note that in America the slash is *not* used to separate apartment numbers from unit numbers in street addresses. For example:

Apt 16, Unit 8 Main St *or* Apt # 16, 8 Main St
or 16, 8 Main St

not 16/8 Main St

Fractions and money

The slash is used mathematically to express fractions. In this context, it is often referred to as a 'scratch'. For example:

½ ¾ 9/10

It is also used after an amount of money, to make clear the precise amount and prevent extra digits being added. For example:

$45/- $6200/- $80 000/-

Line ends

The slash is used to indicate line breaks when quoting from poetry and plays. This is the only time the slash is spaced. For example:

> Had we but world enough, and time, / This coyness, Lady, were no crime.
>
> Andrew Marvell, 'To his coy mistress'

Where *not* to use the slash

The slash is best avoided in formal writing, as it is considered bad form. In particular, do not use it in the following three situations.

First, do not use the slash to separate two-letter initialisms. For example:

> black-and-white *not* b/w
>
> weekend *not* w/e
>
> without *not* w/o

Second, do not use the slash to indicate spans of time (the en rule is correct). For example:

> 60 000–10 000 BC *not* 60 000/10 000 BC
>
> the 2007–08 financial year *not* the 2007/08 financial year

Third, do not use the slash to link two words together, or indicate an association between them (as above, the en rule is correct). For example:

> Muslim–Jewish relations *not* Muslim/Jewish relations
>
> the Archway–Highgate area *not* the Archway/Highgate area

Writing inclusively

Ms: despite the derision that greeted its early users in the 1950s … has proved a blessing to everyone, men and women alike, in avoiding the need to research into or divine the personal circumstances of female addressees.

HW Fowler, Modern English Usage, *p. 411*

One aspect of writing that is regularly debated is inclusive or non-discriminatory writing, and how best to achieve it. As often, the challenge lies not so much in knowing *what* to do as in knowing *how* to do it. We may be well aware that inclusive writing is that which does not exclude or discriminate against individuals or groups, yet how to achieve it without resorting to cumbersomely grammatical sentences, or sentences striving so earnestly to be politically correct that they sound like a spoof?

Here are some strategies.

Gender neutrality

Much of the discussion about sexist language centres round the word 'man' used in the generic sense of 'men and women', and the implied imbalance between the sexes. To help display equal respect towards both men and women, avoid nouns or adjectives containing the prefix '-man'. For example:

artificial *rather than* man-made

humanity *rather than* mankind

labour or workforce *rather than* manpower

Job descriptions are riddled with sexism, often unconscious, since many occupations traditionally performed by men are now carried out also by women. So, stress the role itself rather than the gender of the person performing it, and avoid using the suffix '-man'. For example:

firefighter *rather than* fireman

police officer *rather than* policeman

supervisor *rather than* foreman

In the same way, avoid descriptions of jobs that contain the word 'master'. For example:

compere *rather than* master of ceremonies

expert mason *rather than* master mason

mechanic-in-charge *rather than* master mechanic

Avoid descriptions of jobs that apply exclusively to women, particularly those with the suffix '-ess'. For example:

actor *rather than* actress

flight attendant *rather than* stewardess

host *rather than* hostess

The same applies to roles that used to be the preserve of women, but are no longer. For example:

dancer *rather than* male dancer

nurse *rather than* male nurse

teacher *rather than* male teacher

Using the suffix '-person' can offer a way around this, although some terms sound too contrived to be readily embraced. In this case, simply describe the role rather than the person doing it. For example:

athlete *rather than* sportsperson

chair, convenor *or* leader *rather than* chairperson

sales assistant *rather than* salesperson

Finally, avoid gratuitous reference to people's marital status. For example:

divorced *rather than* divorcee

partner *rather than* husband *or* wife

single *rather than* unmarried

Pronouns

Avoid using the male pronoun 'he' (or 'himself' and 'his') to represent both sexes. This represents a persistent challenge in business documents. For example:

When the user logs on to the system, he must use the correct password.

There are various ways to change this to avoid using a male pronoun.

First, use the plural form:

When users log on, they must use the correct password.

Second, use the personal pronoun 'you':

When you log on, you must use the correct password.

Third, refer to 'he/she' or s/he'. For example:

When the user logs on, he/she (or s/he) must use the correct password.

Fourth, turn the sentence around and rephrase it. For example:

> Make sure your password is correct when you log on.

Fifth, repeat the noun, if necessary splitting the sentence in two and fleshing one of them out to avoid two excessively short sentences. For example:

> The user logs on to the system. Note that the user must use the correct password.

* * *

A word of caution in our pursuit of non-sexist language: many English words, taken from Old English and Latin, have their origins in a time which was male-dominated, indeed sexist by modern standards, and it would be a pity to lose perfectly good expressions because of their etymology.

For instance, take the word 'master' which derives from the Latin *magister*, meaning 'teacher' or 'master', reflecting a time when teachers were predominantly male (although its feminine version, *magistra*, also existed). This word plays a part in many modern expressions, some of which are easily rephrased using a neutral term (e.g. 'main bedroom' rather than 'master bedroom'). Yet other expressions have no neutral alternative and if we cease to use them purely because they contain the word 'master', our vocabulary stands to become that little bit poorer (e.g. why replace the concise verb 'to mastermind' with its laborious definition, 'to plan and direct activities skilfully'?).

We encounter a similar problem in ancient texts and much of pre-1970 literature, as well as many of the proverbs spawned by both. For example:

> Man cannot live by bread alone
>
> Deuteronomy viii:3; Matthew iv:4

lacks rhythm if rephrased

> People cannot live by bread alone *or* one cannot live by bread alone.

The same applies to this much-quoted line:

> No man is an island …
>
> John Donne, *Devotions upon Emergent Occasions*, Meditation 17, 1624

which is diminished as

> No person is an island *or* no one is an island.

Happily, rephrasing a quote does not always lessen its impact. For example:

> Men are so simple, and so much creatures of circumstance, that the deceiver will always find someone ready to be deceived
>
> Niccolò Machiavelli, *The Prince*, XVIII, p. 100

sounds fine as

> People are so simple, and so much creatures of circumstance, that the deceiver will always find someone ready to be deceived

(although substituting 'people' for 'men' ignores the fact that Machiavelli was targeting men hoping to gain and hold onto power in the turbulent world of Florentine Renaissance politics).

It becomes trickier when pronouns are involved—and nowhere is this truer than in Machiavelli's pronoun-strewn text. For example:

> Men worry less about doing an injury to one who makes himself loved than to one who makes himself feared
>
> Niccolò Machiavelli, *The Prince*, XVII, p. 96

which becomes clumsy as

> People worry less about doing an injury to one who makes himself or herself loved than to one who makes himself or herself feared

and vague if we resort to plurals, as

> People worry less about doing an injury to those who make themselves loved than to those who make themselves feared.

With older sayings and proverbs in particular, gender neutrality may have to be bought at the expense of elegance as well as grammar. This proverb, for example:

> Every man for himself

is ungainly as

> Every man or woman (or person) for himself or herself

and ungrammatical as

> Every person for themself.

In such cases, it makes sense to be aware of the context in which something was conceived, and accept 'man' in the generic sense of applying to both men and women.

Ethnic diversity

Stereotyping of people's ethnic and cultural background and gratuitous references to it are common manifestations of lack of respect for ethnic diversity.

Stereotypes and cultural clichés

Imagine that, instead of being yourself, you are the person you're addressing or referring to, and ask yourself how your words might feel. We all see things through a prism shaped by our own culture, age and experience of life, and we are often not aware of our own attitudes until we see them through someone else's eyes. Without an ability to empathise with another's perspective, we remain open to the risk of perpetuating prejudices and stereotypes.

This comment, for example, illustrates how a wrong assumption in an off-the-cuff remark—or a deliberate attempt at clichéd humour—can have a deep effect:

> I got married some years ago. I am originally from the Philippines, and my husband is Australian. A television personality who happened to catch sight of our wedding while he was covering a nearby cricket match commented that I was a 'mail-order bride'. The remark sparked a long debate, and finally an apology, but I was never quite sure that the commentator really understood what it feels like to be talked about in that way …

Many lesser comments pass unnoticed, and are in a way more insidious. The same woman, for instance, notes people's surprise when she explains that, far from applying to enter the country, she was recruited here on account of her professional skills; another woman notes how, when making business calls, a small percentage of clients regularly assume that she is the secretary rather than a partner in the business, thus blurring assumptions about ethnic background with the broader issue of gender equality.

Gratuitous references to ethnic background

Unless directly relevant, there is no need to refer to a person's ethnic background. We are all of ethnic origin, and the terms 'British', 'American', 'Canadian', 'South African', 'Australian' and 'New Zealand' cover all citizens, including those of migrant descent born overseas or whose parents were born overseas. For example:

> The lawyer won her case
> *not* the Croatian-born lawyer won her case.

In specific contexts, references to ethnic backgrounds may be pertinent, or indeed necessary. Should you be discussing legal cases won by Croatian-born lawyers, for instance, the second part of the example would be justified.

Take, however, the case of a couple from Croatia recently arrived in Australia with limited English in search of a lawyer with whom they can communicate. The ethnic background of lawyers is relevant, yet reference can be made to their descent without defining them exclusively in terms of their country of ethnic origin. For example:

> the firm has a Croatian–Australian lawyer *or* the firm has a Croatian-speaking lawyer
> *rather than* the firm has a Croatian lawyer.

Note: In Australia, 'Aboriginal' is used as a noun and an adjective rather than 'Aborigine', although 'Aboriginal and Torres Strait Islander peoples' is preferable. 'Indigenous' is another broad term that refers to the original inhabitants of Australia and uses a capital 'I' (e.g. 'Indigenous affairs'), whereas 'indigenous' with a lower-case 'i' refers to a race or species that originates in or is typical of a particular area (e.g. 'the plants are indigenous to India').

Disabilities

Avoid referring to people primarily in terms of their disability, as if this were their defining characteristic. To do so is insulting as well as inaccurate. For instance, to describe the late theoretical physicist Stephen Hawkins as 'the disabled scientist' on account of his motor neurone disease is patently ridiculous.

Many less dramatic examples of this sort of labelling exist, as evidenced in this type of everyday comment:

> Who's that kid? Oh, he's the one with the heart condition.
>
> She's a quadriplegic, but an accomplished artist.
>
> Go and ask the lame man at number eight—maybe he noticed.

Such statements are condescending and include information which—specific contexts aside—is irrelevant. They can easily be rephrased objectively. For example:

> Who's that kid? Oh, he's Joe. (*unless discussing which child has a heart condition*)
>
> She's an accomplished artist. (*unless citing disability as being no barrier to accomplishment*)
>
> Go and ask the man at number eight—maybe he noticed. (*unless several men live at number eight and only one is both lame and observant*)

Always put the individual before the disability, and remember that the same disability can affect different people in different ways. For example:

> a person with a disability *rather than* a crippled, deformed, disabled or handicapped person
>
> a person with a hearing difficulty *rather than* a deaf person
>
> a person with epilepsy *rather than* an epileptic

Avoid using euphemisms such as 'challenged', 'differently abled' and 'inconvenienced'. For example:

> a person who wears glasses *rather than* a visually challenged person
>
> a person who is partly paralysed *rather than* a differently abled person
>
> a person who walks with crutches *rather than* a physically inconvenienced person

Use neutral, non-emotional terms to describe people with disabilities. For example:

> a person who has had a heart attack *rather than* a heart attack victim

a person with arthritis *rather than* a person suffering from, or afflicted with, arthritis

a wheelchair user *rather than* a person confined or restricted to a wheelchair

Where the disability is developmental, cognitive or emotional rather than physical, avoid inaccurate or derogatory expressions. For example:

a person with a developmental disability *rather than* a slow learner

a person with a cognitive disability *rather than* a retarded or subnormal person, or spastic

a person with an emotional disability *rather than* a crazy or paranoid person, or nutter

If possible, be specific and name the disability. For example:

a person with bipolar disorder *is more specific than* a person with an emotional disability

a person with Down syndrome *is more specific than* a person with a developmental disability

a person with dyslexia *is more specific than* a person with a cognitive disability

Finally, when referring to people without disabilities, try to avoid terms such as 'able-bodied', 'healthy', 'normal' or 'whole' person—all of which imply that any variation is necessarily inferior.

Age

The demographics of western society are changing rapidly: a few hundred years ago 40 was considered old, whereas now, as the saying goes, life begins at 40—or 50. Ours is an ageing society, and the average age is set to increase. According to a study conducted in

2017 by the United Nations,[1] the number of older people (broadly defined as over 60) is expected to more than double by 2050 and the trend, currently headed by Europe, will be largely irreversible. It is important to bear this in mind when considering how to address your readership.

Always put the person before the label, and see individuals' qualities before their age bracket. Just as an attitude that stereotypes people according to gender or ethnic origin is considered sexist or racist, an attitude that stereotypes people according to age rather than individual abilities, known as 'ageism', is discriminatory.

Avoid making gratuitous reference to a person's age. Such references are particularly common in the area of employment. For example:

> He's an older man and a very experienced operator.
>
> That smartly dressed middle-aged woman is the new director.
>
> We hired a young assistant to help you.

Statements like these can easily be rephrased objectively. For example:

> He's a very experienced operator. (*unless you are citing age as proof of experience*)
>
> That smartly-dressed woman is the new boss. (*unless you are in a roomful of smartly-dressed women and only one is middle-aged*)
>
> We hired an assistant to help you. (*unless the assistant's age is under discussion*)

[1] United Nations, 'World Population Prospects: the 2017 Revision', viewed 4 March 2018, http://www.un.org/en/sections/issues-depth/ageing/

'Young' and 'old' are relative terms, each loaded with connotation. Where possible, use neutral terms. For example, refer to:

adolescents *or* young people *rather than* teenagers or youths

women *rather than* girls (*unless very young*)

mature *rather than* middle-aged

retired *or* senior citizens *rather than* aged, elderly or old

The changing demographics have an obvious impact on written documents in terms of design. The principles of good design that apply to all documents can be tailored in subtle ways to suit older readers in the following ways.

Typeface design

Use typefaces with maximum legibility (i.e. where each letter or word is easily recognised). Simple typefaces with a consistent density of letterform strokes are more legible than cursive, decorative ones. Serif typefaces are more legible than sans serif ones because the ascenders and descenders of lower-case letters help us recognise the shapes of words (which is why Times, Garamond and Palatino remain universal favourites).

Type size

Use big type sizes for greater visibility (14 point or larger is ideal for body text; 12 point is the minimum). Avoid extra fine, narrow or compressed fonts.

Leading

Use generous leading (i.e. the space inserted between lines of type, originally designed to prevent any overlap between the descenders of one line and the ascenders of the line below). Long lines and squat, chunky typefaces with short ascenders and descenders (typical of many sans serif fonts) are made more easily legible with extra leading.

Line length

Ensure that the average line length is approximately 10–12 words (or 65 character spaces). Longer lines reduce our reading speed and we tend to give up more quickly, although extra leading helps.

Capitals and italics

Avoid strings of capitals or italics, which are hard to read. Capitals and italics work well for single lines, such as headings or captions, but are harder to read than lower-case letters or Roman typefaces when used for multiple lines or whole paragraphs.

In addition, if you're writing material designed to be read on-screen, keep these points in mind.

Navigation

Ensure that the navigation system is clear, and that there is a tool or site map enabling readers to remain aware of where they are in the overall structure. This is crucial in long documents where readers have to scroll down to reach the end. We tend to scan on-screen material far more than we do printed matter: rather than following the text sequentially, we instinctively look first at the centre, then at the left and right sides before scrolling down to the end. The 'scannability' of on-screen documents therefore assumes greater importance.

Typeface

Use sans serif typefaces which, with their uniform thickness of strokes in all letters, suit the screen better than serif typefaces (e.g. Arial and Helvetica are popular).

Unjustified text

Use unjustified (or ragged right) text. Although not as neat as justified text, blocks of unjustified text are easier to read, whether or not the line ends are hyphenated. Avoid centring text where possible; single lines work fine, but whole blocks of centred text are hard to read.

Columns

Avoid using two or more columns. Columns of text are difficult to read on-screen, especially when we have to scroll up and down.

Paragraphs

Use block paragraphs (i.e. paragraphs separated by a line space, with first lines full out) rather than indented ones, as they are easier to scan.

Emphasis

Use bold rather than italics for emphasis, as bold is more effective on-screen.

Backgrounds

Ensure there is sufficient contrast between the words and their background (this is a risk when text appears against coloured panels).

Copyright

Only one thing is impossible for God: To find any sense in any copyright law on the planet.

Mark Twain, Mark Twain's Notebook, *1902–03, prepared by AB Paine, Harper & Brothers Publishers, New York, 1935*

Definition

Copyright is a legal concept designed to protect original literary, dramatic, musical and artistic works from unlawful reproduction, and encourage the creation of new works. Novels, poems, plays, films, song lyrics, paintings, drawings, plans, cartoons and photos are commonly cited examples of works in copyright, but articles, reports, computer programs, compilations, sound recordings and broadcasts are also covered.

Note that literary value is *not* part of the requirements of copyright, and that creations such as databases and timetables as well as letters and emails are included in the 'literary works' category, as long as they are original and not utterly trivial. Whether a work is subsequently published or not has no bearing on its copyright status.

Ideas v. expression

Copyright does not protect ideas or information but rather the manner of their expression. For example, you can refer to or explain Edward de Bono's thinking strategies with due acknowledgment, but not recount a substantial portion of them *in his original words* (or display his accompanying drawings) unless you clear permission to quote him directly (or reproduce his drawings).

This distinction between ideas and their expression, which lies at the very heart of copyright, is open to interpretation and has, predictably, led to many a dispute. At what point can a draft be said to reach tangible form? To what degree can a work be said to be derivative? Are several words sufficient to be protected?

Copyright is a complex field; should you have any concern when quoting even a short piece of material, seek early clarification from your country's copyright agency.

Who owns the copyright?

Copyright is automatic, free, and exists from the moment a work is created in tangible form (i.e. written, recorded or made). It is usually the creator of a work who owns the copyright, although there are exceptions. For instance, if a work is done by an employee on behalf of an employer, the employer usually retains the copyright; if a work is commissioned, the individual or institution who commissioned it usually holds the copyright rather than the artist who created it.

Note that owning the copyright to a work is distinct from owning the physical form in which that work exists. For example, owning an original Dickens manuscript does not mean that you own the copyright to it or can reproduce it.

Copyright laws

Each country has its own copyright laws, detailed in their own Copyright Acts, to which there are regular amendments.

In addition, copyright material is protected internationally. All English-speaking countries are members of a global network of copyright agreements.

The Berne Convention, dating from 1886, established that copyright applies automatically from the moment a work is created (that is, it is not something for which its author need apply). It also ensured that foreign authors were to be accorded the same copyright protection as national authors.

The World Intellectual Property Organisation Copyright Treaty, set up in 1996, (known as the WIPO Copyright Treaty) offered additional protection for material created as a result of information technology, such as computer programs and databases.

These principles in practice now apply internationally despite some differences between copyright laws as enacted in various countries.

Rights of the copyright holder

As one of the forms of 'intellectual property' (the other main ones being patents, trademarks and designs), copyright confers on the holder certain 'exclusive rights' over a work, depending on its nature. These consist of the right to publish, reproduce, distribute, sell or export it, to adapt it, to display or perform it—as well as the right to refuse others permission to reproduce or use it in any way, including by photocopying or scanning or, in the case of a computer program, hiring it out. The copyright holder also retains the right to assign the copyright to someone else, including selling it, or to license someone else to use it.

Copyright holders also enjoy what is referred to as 'moral rights'; that is, the right to protect their reputation in connection with their copyrighted material. This is usually used by authors to ensure correct attribution, defend themselves against false attribution, and defend themselves against derogatory treatment (also referred to as the 'right of integrity').

'Substantial' material

It is the author's responsibility to obtain permission to reproduce any 'substantial' material, ensure that it is presented in accordance with the wishes of the copyright holder/s, and pay any associated fees.

Material is defined as being 'substantial' in terms of its essential value to the whole work: it is a measure of quality, not quantity. Even a few lines may be deemed 'substantial' if they are distinctive or capture the essence of a work. Tables, charts and diagrams also fall into this category.

Although publishing houses often devise an in-house barometer of this substantive value in terms of length (usually 80–400 words), remember that this should be seen as supporting the notion of 'essential to the whole' rather than replacing it. A few lines can be considered 'substantial', whereas a paragraph of 200 words may not—if those words are of interest to the text, but not essential.

Fair dealing

The Copyright Acts of most countries make various provisions for 'fair dealing' (termed 'fair use' in America) in the sense of fair-minded and genuine rather than simply non-profit. This allows for a 'reasonable' amount of material (about 10 per cent or one chapter of a printed book or electronic work, whichever is longer) to be reproduced copyright-free, with full acknowledgment, for particular purposes.

The purposes behind writing covered by fair dealing include:

- research or study (e.g. textbooks or study guides)
- criticism or review (e.g. literary criticism or analysis)
- reporting news (e.g. newspapers or magazines)
- parody or satire (e.g. a humorous imitation or commentary)
- providing access to people with a disability.

In all purposes, however, the context in which you use your material and your purpose in using it have a greater bearing on an assessment of whether it is 'fair' than its length. For example, for the purpose of criticism and review, you can include a quote in order to give a critical evaluation of the ideas within it or review them, but not for ulterior motives such as commercial benefit alone.

The duration of copyright

Literary, dramatic and musical works that have been published remain in copyright for 70 years after the death of the creator, after which copyright is transferred to that person's estate. If those works have not been published, performed, displayed or recorded, they remain in copyright indefinitely.

Artistic works, including photos, remain in copyright for 70 years after the death of the creator, regardless of whether they have been published or not.

If 70 years have elapsed and the work you're reproducing is out of copyright, or 'insubstantial', you must still acknowledge your source in full. For a written work, this typically includes the author, the title of publication in which the material appears, the publisher, the place of publication, the year of publication and the page number.

Requesting permission

It is best to obtain permission to use copyright material in written form, and ensure that the letter granting permission is signed by the copyright holder (which makes it legally binding). It is therefore important to keep accurate and detailed records of all the material you use, both text and illustrations. This is crucial with indirect sources such as the Internet, where a screening process is not inbuilt and where it is up to the user to evaluate and validate information.

When drawing up a permissions request, give the copyright holder full details of what you wish to reproduce, and why, and the publication in which you wish to reproduce it. If possible, include the page where the copyright material will appear to show the context in which you wish to use it. Note that the original must be faithfully reproduced in every respect, including any errors (indicated by using the Latin [*sic*], meaning 'thus').

For published material, the publishing house is usually the copyright holder (if not, it should be able to inform you who is); for unpublished material, the author usually owns the copyright.

Note: Refer to the Appendix for a permissions request template that you can copy and tailor to your individual needs.

Acknowledgment lines

Once permission is granted and any conditions met, a formal acknowledgment should be made. (In the case of books this includes author, year of publication, title, publisher, place of publication and page number.) You can do this either in a single credit line beneath the material itself or, if there are multiple credits, gathered as part of an acknowledgments section with an expression of gratitude, if appropriate. For example:

> Source: *The New Yorker*, January 21, 2018
> Reproduced by kind permission of Marina Cadiz (*single credit*)
>
> The following sources are gratefully acknowledged: JE Heerse (ed.), *The Journal of Tasman* (p. 57); the *Melbourne Punch* for Chevalier's cartoon, 1865 (p. 35); … (*multiple credits*)

Copyright page

Also referred to as the imprint page or reverse title page, the copyright page displays your own copyright line, together with full bibliographical details of your own work. The copyright line contains the copyright symbol © followed by the author's name (or that of an incorporated body) and the year of first publication, with no intervening commas. (Note that any authoring body must be a legal entity in order to own copyright; therefore, a business name, not being a legal entity, cannot, whereas a company can.) For example:

© Mila Petrović 1999

© National Library of New Zealand 2017

A more detailed copyright notice can follow, such as that inserted by most publishing houses. Although there is no prescribed text, it is usually worded along these lines:

> This work is copyright. Apart from any use permitted under the *(name of appropriate Copyright Act)*, no part may be reproduced, stored in a retrieval system or transmitted in any form or by any means, electronic, mechanical, photocopying, recording or otherwise, without the prior written permission of (*name of publisher or copyright owner*).

Note: The words 'All rights reserved' sometimes appear as the opening line, or even as a stand-alone line, particularly in American publications.

Although protection of a work does not require the presence of the copyright line or notice and exists equally without it, it is wise to include it as an internationally recognisable reminder that material is under copyright. Also, should unauthorised reproduction of material lead to a lawsuit, the presence of a copyright line and notice make it less tenable for the defence to claim 'innocent infringement'.

If copyright has been infringed and there is a dispute, the matter could ultimately go to court, although this is rare because of the potentially high costs incurred. Nevertheless, it is pragmatic to keep a dated draft or copy of your work, as well as of any related correspondence, as proof of authorship.

Plagiarism

When you take stuff from one writer, it's plagiarism. But when you take it from many writers, it's research.

Attributed to Wilson Mizner, American playwright and raconteur (1876–1933)

Plagiarism is the taking of someone else's original words or ideas and presenting them as one's own, whether by direct appropriation or close imitation. Our word 'plagiarism' derives from the Latin *plagiarius*, meaning 'kidnapper', 'plunderer' or, as the first-century Roman poet Martial put it, 'literary thief'.

Plagiarism can take various forms:

- copying word for word someone else's text and presenting it as your own (the most obvious form of plagiarism)
- copying a significant amount of someone else's text with token changes—usually by altering a few key words or phrases—and presenting it as your own
- paraphrasing or expressing someone else's essential idea and presenting it as your own
- paraphrasing essential ideas from multiple sources, weaving them together, and presenting them as your own
- copying your own previously produced words or ideas without explaining the context in which they were originally written, or remoulding them to suit a new audience (i.e. self-plagiarism)

- inadvertently copying someone else's words or ideas (i.e. accidental or unintentional plagiarism)
- giving an incomplete or inaccurate source for a quote, including unintentionally (e.g. giving the author's name but omitting a full reference)
- neglecting to make clear precisely where a direct quote begins and ends, which includes omitting quote marks.

Internet publishing has made plagiarism easier to do and harder to detect. The cut-and-paste tool, so invaluable in writing and editing, is unfortunately seen by some as an invitation to online plagiarism. Furthermore, attempts to manipulate search engines to duplicate another person's content and re-present it as one's own are leading to a growing problem of 'content scraping' or 'content theft'. Various plagiarism-detection devices and software do exist to detect and prevent online plagiarism, but they tend to work only for the most obvious word-for-word copies.

So, keep track of all your sources, both printed and online. Make sure you get your citations correct and provide a comprehensive bibliography.

Plagiarism is often mentioned in connection with copyright, although the two are essentially different. Plagiarism is concerned with stealing another's words or ideas and is a form of intellectual theft; copyright is concerned with the protection of the rights of the copyright holder.

Slander and libel may also be mentioned, although they too are quite different from plagiarism. Slander consists of malicious, false spoken words; libel arises from false words or statements that are published or permanently recorded and are damaging to a person's reputation. The terms are often used interchangeably despite the legal difference.

It is important to understand that any claims or accusations must be able to be substantiated. If you make a claim about someone and that person sues you, the onus is on you to prove it rather than on the other person to disprove it.

PART TWO:
Manuscript Presentation

The role of the computer

The newest computer can merely compound, at speed, the oldest problem in the relations between human beings, and in the end the communicator will be confronted with the old problem, of what to say and how to say it.

Edward R Murrow, American broadcast journalist, 1964

Anyone working with words can be seduced by the variety of desktop publishing packages available. With so much technical sophistication at our collective fingertips, it is easy to get distracted by how the text 'looks'. The word-processor, like the typewriter before it, facilitates the act of putting ideas down on paper and editing them, but not necessarily the formation of those ideas. Most of us approach our work differently when we work directly onto the computer.

A revealing exercise is to compare, say, a page of your hard copy revisions (i.e. using pen and paper) with your on-screen ones. You may find subtle differences between the two versions, so be aware of this when planning how to work.

Some people work exclusively on the computer; others prefer hard copy. For most of us, a balance between the two serves us best. You may find it natural, for example, to print out a first draft and then use pen and paper to make your revisions before taking in your final changes on-screen. Working out a combination of computer and pen and paper that suits you is a prerequisite for effective writing.

Choose an approach that helps you concentrate on your content, keeping its presentation as simple as possible.

Whether you choose to edit exclusively on-screen or partly on hard copy, it is wise to have a print-out of your final, complete manuscript.

Here are some basic guidelines to follow when printing out your manuscript—which will also, incidentally, ensure that it conforms to the presentation listed by those publishers or literary agents who request hard copy submissions.

Typing and spacing

Use A4 paper, and print on one side only. Use one-and-a-half or double spacing throughout, including for any quotes, tables, notes or references. This allows plenty of space for editorial revisions.

If possible, avoid having the first line of a new paragraph fall at the bottom of a page (known as an 'orphan') or the last line of the previous paragraph fall at the top of the next page (known as a 'widow'). Single, floating lines are visually distracting. In both cases, try to keep at least two lines together.

Avoid attaching last-minute alterations or instructions to your manuscript, as they can be confusing and are easily lost. If you need to make late insertions, add them alphabetically (e.g. page 14a, b or c), and remember to update your electronic copy accordingly.

Indicate a new paragraph by indenting the first line rather than leaving an extra line space (to avoid ambiguity should a new paragraph fall at the top of a page). Do not, however, indent the first line of a displayed quote or of text immediately following a heading, both of which are clearer ranged left (referred to as 'full out').

Allow a minimum of 2.5 cm (or just under an inch) for margins, both top and bottom and at either side.

Formatting

Keep formatting to a minimum. There is no need to justify the text or introduce typographical refinements. If you have more than one level of heading, indicate their relative importance either by grading them '1', '2' or '3' or by inserting 'A', 'B' or 'C' before each one (three should be a maximum). If you wish to differentiate them visually, do so as simply as possible (e.g. use bold rather than an ornate capitalised font).

Pagination

Number pages consecutively rather than by chapter, section or part. This is primarily for ease of working; should the manuscript be dropped or the pages become mixed up it makes them easier to re-order. For the same reason, write 'end' clearly at the bottom of the final page of your manuscript.

Use a fresh page to indicate the start of each new chapter, section or part. When printed, these will become right-hand pages displaying odd numbers, with left-hand pages having even numbers (this is known as 'paginating', as opposed to 'foliating' where only the front side of each page, or folio, is numbered). Also use a fresh page to accommodate material such as a table that has to be presented as a single entity on one page, be it a right-hand page (referred to as a 'recto') or a left-hand page (referred to as a 'verso').

Ideally, use lower-case roman numerals (e.g. i, ii, iii) for preliminary pages (known as 'prelims' (which include the title page, foreword, contents, preface and acknowledgments). Use arabic numerals (e.g. 1, 2, 3) for the start of the text (that is, with the introduction, if there is one, or with the first chapter). This allows the prelims to be added to or changed at any point without affecting the pagination of the rest of the manuscript.

Correct sequence of parts

A book is composed of three main segments: the preliminary matter (*prelims* or *front matter*), the text, and the endmatter. Each of these is in turn composed of certain items, subject to a given order and presentation.

R Ritter, The Oxford Guide to Style,
Oxford University Press, 2002, p. 1

The components of a publication generally follow this order, although in smaller books—like this one—some elements may not be present and their order may vary slightly.

Preliminary pages

These use roman numerals, and each component takes a recto (right-hand page), with the verso (left-hand page) left blank if necessary. They include:

- **half-title page**, p. i (optional, and contains the main title)
- **title page**, p. iii (contains the main title, subtitle, author/editor, and publisher)
- **imprint page**, p. iv (contains the publishing history and copyright information; also displays the dedication if there is one, which is placed at the top of the page in a larger type size)
- **foreword** (optional, and written by someone other than author/editor to explain the purpose of the book)

- **contents** (lists the chapter headings, main headings and sometimes also the subheadings; also lists the prelims and endmatter)
- **list of illustrations and tables** (optional, depending on the audience)
- **preface** (written by the author/s or editor/s to explain how and why the book was written; prefaces to new editions outline the nature of the changes)
- **acknowledgments** (credits those who assisted in preparing the book, and is best kept succinct and within one page; it can also be placed discreetly at the end of the book).

Text

This uses arabic numerals, and each main component takes a new page. It includes:

- **introduction**, p. 1 (expands on the preface, including essential or relevant background information; non-essential information is included in the preface)
- **text** (divided into chapters and possibly parts or sections).

Endmatter

This continues the arabic numerals, and each main component takes a new page. It includes:

- **appendix** (contains supplementary material that is too detailed or technical to include in the text, or that is of indirect interest to it rather than critical)
- **glossary** (lists technical or unfamiliar terms in alphabetical order and gives short definitions)

- **references or endnotes** (give full details of publications cited in the text, including page numbers if appropriate)
- **bibliography** (lists the publications used or cited in the text; can also include recommended reading)
- **index** (contains a level of detail enabling the reader to locate particular areas of interest; includes specialised indexes such as Name index or Place index).

Style sheets

A foolish consistency is the hobgoblin of little minds, adored by little statesmen and philosophers and divines.

Ralph Waldo Emerson, American essayist, philosopher and poet (1803–1882), Essays: First Series *(published 1841 as* Essays*), 'Self-reliance'*

And editors, Ralph Waldo Emerson might have added. At an early stage in your writing, it is wise to draw up what is known as an editorial 'style sheet', the purpose of which is precisely to ensure stylistic consistency. For a brief document, it is one of the most useful reference tools a writer can have. It is, in essence, a form on which you record your policy on variant spellings including capitalisation and hyphenation, as well as the presentation of elements such as headings, lists, quotes, tables, illustrations and bibliographical material.

Editorial departments of publishing houses regularly compile style sheets for their manuscripts to ensure that the stylistic conventions favoured by that company (commonly referred to as 'house style') are uniformly applied across all books. Most publishing houses incorporate a style sheet within their own in-house style guides which they hand out to authors and copy editors under contract.

From a writer's point of view, the style sheet functions as a prompt and accessible reminder of how to deal with matters of style big and small. It is easy to realise, in the course of writing your manuscript, that you've forgotten how you spelled a word (did you use the 's' or 'z' spelling? did you hyphenate it or use an initial capital?), or presented a symbol (did you use the '%' sign or spell out 'per cent'?). Similarly, you may wonder how you presented lists (did you use bullets or numbers?) or quotes (did you display them, or incorporate them into the surrounding text?). If you're working with others, the communicability of a style sheet is a prerequisite to efficient teamwork.

Style sheets are primarily used for nonfiction manuscripts, but in fiction writing too the spelling section can prove helpful.

Here is an example of a partially completed style sheet, in this case for a manuscript on film sound and music.

STYLE SHEET

Title: *Sound Design and Music in Film-Making: Theory and Practice*

ABC	DEF
adviser audiovisual avant-garde -based (e.g. loss-based) Bergman, Ingmar	decision-making Fassbinder, Rainer Werner film-maker focused, focusing freeze-frame (noun)
GHI	**JKL**
gebrauchsmusik grown-up (noun and adj.) intertextual	judgment a licence (noun) to license (verb)
MNO	**PQR**
mike *not* mic (microphone) mise en scène *Nosferatu*	play-acting post-production pre-production remaster replay
STUV	**WXYZ**
semi-documentary soundtrack stand-alone time frame voice-over	well-known (adj.) whitefella word play

STYLE SHEET, cont.

Headings: 3 levels (Chapter, A, B). Questions to be displayed (interview section).

Lists: Bullet: minimal punctuation (lower case, no full stop)

Quotations: Short ones incorporated into text. Longer ones displayed. Dialogue scripts to be distinguished from textual quotes.

Illustrations: 23 black-and-white photos supplied. Crop as marked, and heighten tonal contrast as required. Captions to be designed.

Footnotes/notes: Superscript numbers in text, and notes at end of each chapter.

Bibliographical references: At the end of each chapter.

Other: Detailed list of contributors to appear in prelims.

Note: Refer to the Appendix for a style sheet template that you can copy and tailor to your individual needs.

Headings

Headings are fundamental to textual contrast: they are signposts for readers. To be effective, they must be carefully graded, distributed and worded.

Style Manual for Authors, Editors and Printers, *p. 137*

A successful heading flags what is important to your readers and holds their attention, as well as informing them of its relative grading within the overall hierarchy. Make your headings interesting, therefore, as well as informative.

Language of headings

The most effective headings are clear and concise, and preferably contained within a single line. They are also best when expressing a single fact or concept rather than trying to make multiple points. For example:

> The reconstruction of agriculture in the postwar period

is easier to absorb than

> The reconstruction of agriculture in the postwar period and its place in a rapidly industrialising economy

although sometimes a duality of purpose may be necessary and, if reasonably concise, can still be clear. For example:

> Rice surpluses and production adjustment

> Targets for self-sufficiency ratios and implied import requirements

In certain contexts, a humorous touch and a direct, conversational tone can help convey a message. For example:

> Fixing photos where you wish you hadn't used the flash

is more appealing than

> How to adjust photos where the flash has been inappropriately used

Headings phrased as questions can be highly effective, especially when there is a sequence of shortish paragraphs exploring parallel themes. This technique works particularly well for popular subjects or younger readers. For example:

> Why is a female cat called a queen?
>
> Why is a male cat called a tom?

Grading headings

The number of heading levels required depends on subject matter and audience. A book on strategic leadership for executives, for example, will use more heading levels than an introductory student text on business management. Fiction rarely requires any headings other than chapter headings, although there are exceptions.

In addition to chapter titles (graded 'Chapter headings'), a typical nonfiction book might use two or three levels of subheading (graded 'A heading', 'B heading' and so forth), all of which can be comfortably reflected in the contents page. Within your manuscript, grade each heading, whether electronically or on hard copy. For example:

(Ch. hd)	Graphology: The science of handwriting analysis
(A hd)	The origins of graphology
(B hd)	Variations in script size
(C hd)	Large script
(C hd)	Small script

Formatting headings

Keep formatting simple. As writer, your role is to make clear what the levels of headings are rather than design them. Some basic visual differentiation is nevertheless helpful. As a rough guide, use bold for main headings, bold italic for subheadings, and italic for sub-subheadings. Resist experimenting with ornate cursive scripts or embossed, outline or shadow typefaces. Use minimal capitals, as a string of capitals can be hard to read. For example, an A heading in simple bold text typeface such as

Shutter speed and depth of field (*12 pt Arial*)

is more legible than typographical variations such as

Shutter speed and depth of field (*cursive*)

Shutter speed and depth of field (*outline*)

SHUTTER SPEED AND DEPTH OF FIELD (*small caps*)

Leave a single line space above main headings for clarity, range all headings left rather than centring them, and do not place full stops after headings. Range paragraphs left under headings (i.e. don't indent them). Restrict numbering within headings to scientific or technical subjects. For example:

2 Hypothesis testing and reasoning

2.1 Cognitive biases in reasoning and hypothesis testing

2.2 Confirmation bias

Headings that fall at the ends of pages

Avoid headings that fall at the bottom of pages, separated from the text to which they apply. To achieve the desired minimum of two lines of text beneath headings, take a heading over onto the next page and leave the preceding page short.

Contents list

The first known reference to a table of contents is believed to have been that of St Jerome (c. 340–420 AD) who, in his Prologue to the 'Commentary on Isaiah', used the term *capitulum* to refer to numbered chapter headings, and *index capitulorum* to refer to a list of headings.

Consider the contents list as a detailed signpost to the text that follows. It reflects main heading levels—usually two and occasionally, in academic or technical material, a third or even a fourth level. The simpler the contents list, the clearer it is.

Typographically, there is no need to differentiate the contents from the rest of the manuscript, so present it in regular typeface and type size, using minimal capitals, with subheadings indented. Page numbers are dropped in at the final stage.

An example of a contents page that is detailed yet clear follows.

CONTENTS

Quotations

I love quotations because it is a joy to find thoughts one might have, beautifully expressed with much authority by someone recognised wiser than oneself.

Attributed to Marlene Dietrich, German-born actor and singer (1901–1992)

A 'quotation' can be defined as the repeating of either written or spoken words. A carefully chosen and well-placed quote can do much to enhance a text. Some are informative or illustrative; others are chosen for their humour or lyrical value. Whatever their purpose, quotes should complement the surrounding text rather than distract from it.

Preserve the quote

Never alter the wording or punctuation within quotes, even if it doesn't conform to modern conventions or contains errors. In the latter case, use the Latin *sic*, meaning 'thus', italicised within square brackets, directly after the word or phrase to indicate that the error appears in the original. For example:

> We continued our march all day yesterday. The road to Souchez has become a marsh. The planks are no use, they have sunk into the ground and it is impossible not to stumble and fall. The only sounds are the squishing of the mud and the swearing of the men. I mis [*sic*] you all. With love, Matthew
>
> Extract from letter of 17-year old British soldier subsequently reported missing in action, France 1916

Short quotes

Treat brief quotes (up to approximately four lines) or quotes which consist of incomplete sentences as part of the overall phrases in which they are embedded. In British English, single punctuation marks are gradually replacing double ones, which in turn can be used for quotes within quotes. For example:

> She explained that Jungian psychology sees the figure of the witch as 'an embodiment of "the dark side of the *anima*" or female aspect of man'.

American English uses double punctuation marks, and single ones for quotes within quotes. For example:

> She explained that Jungian psychology sees the figure of the witch as "an embodiment of 'the dark side of the *anima*' or female aspect of man."

Long quotes

Introduce substantial quotes, or ones that require emphasis, with a colon. Display each quote on a new line, indented, with a single line space before and after. Known as 'block' quotes, they need no enclosing punctuation marks. For example:

> In ancient China the celebrated first Emperor, Shi Huang-ti (ruled 221–210 BC), founder of the Middle Kingdom, divided his empire into 36 military provinces, each administered by one civil and one military governor.

Drama and poetry

Display dramatic text in the same fashion as long quotes, introducing it with a colon and indenting it. In addition, reproduce the typographical layout (such as spacing and line breaks) which, especially in poetry, is crucial to rhythm. For example:

> A snake came to my water-trough
> On a hot, hot day, and I in pyjamas for the heat,
> To drink there.
>
> DH Lawrence, 'Snake'

Sourcing quotes

Always disclose the full source of your quotes (i.e. author, year of publication, title, publisher, place of publication and page number), and ensure that you're consistent in the manner of their presentation. The Harvard style, or author–date system, is the most popular style of referencing. Although there are variations, in essence it consists of the author's name followed by the date of publication and, if appropriate, a page reference. For example:

> Faith is this paradox, and the individual absolutely cannot make himself intelligible to anybody. (Kierkegaard 1954, p. 81)

Full details would be listed in the bibliography, which in this case would read:

> Kierkegaard, S 1954, *Fear and Trembling*, 2nd edn, trans. W Lowrie, Princeton University Press, Princeton.

If the bibliographical information is too lengthy to be incorporated within the text, or if there is extensive cross-referencing, you can insert superscript numerals after each quote, and include full details of the source in footnotes (placed at the end of individual pages), in endnotes (placed at the end of each chapter or section), or in a list of references (placed at the end of the book). For example:

> Faith is this paradox, and the individual absolutely cannot make himself intelligible to anybody.[2]

The footnotes or endnotes would then contain full details. As there is no need for texts to be listed alphabetically, these references are presented in a slightly different manner from those in a bibliography (i.e. the author's initials precede the family name, and the year of publication appears towards the end of the reference). Here, this would read:

> [2] S Kierkegaard, *Fear and Trembling*, Princeton University Press, Princeton, 1954, p. 81.

Note: For details on presenting references, including the use of 'ibid.' and 'op. cit.' for multiple references to texts already cited, see 'In-text citations, footnotes and endnotes'.

Proper names and titles

‘*Must* a name mean something?’ Alice asked doubtfully.
‘Of course it must,’ Humpty Dumpty said with a short laugh:
‘*my* name means the shape I am—and a good handsome
shape it is, too. With a name like yours, you might be any
shape, almost.’

Lewis Carroll, Through the Looking-Glass *(published 1871),*
Chapter VI

Resist the tendency to overuse capitals to lend greater importance or credibility to names or titles. As a general rule, use initial capitals when referring to specific names and titles, but not in generic or unofficial references.

The following categories are listed in order of the most common first.

Proper names and official titles

For example:

> the Director of Public Prosecutions, the Governor of Illinois (*specific*)
>
> *but* a director, a governor; the directors, the governors (*generic*)

Honorary titles (honorifics)

For example:

Dr Elizabeth Slater, Professor Chandler (*specific*)

but a doctor, a professor; the doctors, the professors (*generic*)

Schools and departments

For example:

the International Language School, the Department of Applied Sciences (*specific*)

but a school, a department; the schools, the departments (*generic*)

Organisations, institutions and centres

For example:

the Royal Bank of Canada, the British Library, the Arab Cultural Centre (*specific*)

but a bank, a library, a centre; the banks, the libraries, the centres (*generic*)

Governments

For example:

the Western Australian Government, the New Zealand Government (*specific*)

but government policy, the succession of governments (*generic*)

Parliaments

For example:

the European Parliament, the Parliament of South Africa (*specific*)

but a parliamentary debate, the parliamentary procedures (*generic*)

Commonwealth

For example:

the Commonwealth of Australia, the Commonwealth of Nations (*specific*)

but many states joining together are said to form a commonwealth (*generic*)

Federal

For example:

the Federal Bureau of Investigation, the Federal Court of Australia (*specific*)

but federal opposition, federal systems (*generic*)

Specific nouns associated with government

For example:

tomorrow's Budget, the government department known as the Treasury (*specific*)

but previous budgets, the companies' treasuries (*generic*)

Geographical names and topographical features

For example:

South-East Asia, the West, the Dead Sea and the Sea of Galilee (*specific*)

but central Asia; western Europe, two seas close together (*generic*)

Significant historical events or movements

For example:

the Vietnam War, Surrealism (*specific*)

but the wars in Vietnam, surrealist painters (*generic*)

Public holidays and important cultural, religious or sporting events

For example:

Thanksgiving Day, St Patrick's Day, the Davis Cup (*specific*)

but commemorative days, patron saints, cup finals (*generic*)

Literary and artistic works

Consistency is only a paste jewel that cheap men cherish.

William A White, American newspaper editor, politician and author (1868–1944)

Do we write *War and Peace* or *War and peace*? Do we write *Schindler's List* or 'Schindler's List'? And how do we properly refer to the title of an essay or article?

There are inevitable discrepancies in the presentation of such titles as recommended by established style manuals, with yet another layer of variety introduced depending on the type of writing; that is, certain conventions apply to general writing, others to medical material, and journalism often develops its own in-house style.

As a general rule, titles of substantial creative works are italicised and take initial capitals for main words; and titles of shorter works, or segments of a whole, take roman type, minimal capitals and single quote marks. This is illustrated in the following examples.

Books

Use italics and initial capitals for main words. For example:

> *Rich Dad, Poor Dad* by RT Kiyosaki was the number one business book in 1998.
>
> *The Island of the Day Before* by Umberto Eco is as whimsical as its title.

Use your discretion about what constitutes a 'main' word in a title. For example, the verb 'did' might or might not be critical, depending on the relative emphasis given to the surrounding words. In the crime novel

Baby did a Bad Bad Thing

it is the 'thing' rather than the 'did' that is the focus, whereas in the classic story

What Katy Did

it is the 'did' that commands our attention.

Chapters within books

Use minimal capitals and quote marks. For example:

> In his chapter 'Why teach financial literacy?' Kiyosaki urges us not to rely on school systems to understand how money works.
>
> See the chapter 'The map of tenderness' in *The Island of the Day Before.*

Essays

Use minimal capitals and quote marks. For example:

> TS Eliot's essay, 'Tradition and the individual talent' is one of the most celebrated critical essays in the English language of the twentieth century.
>
> In her essay 'Against interpretation' Susan Sontag argues for a more sensual, less narrowly intellectual approach to art and culture.

Poems

Use minimal capitals and quote marks for shorter poems, and use italics and minimal capitals for longer poems. For example:

> 'Beach burial', which explores the futility of war, and 'Five bells', which describes Sydney harbour, are two of Kenneth Slessor's most powerful poems.
>
> Coleridge's poem *The rime of the ancient mariner* may have been inspired by Cook's exploratory voyages from 1772–5.

Newspapers

Use italics and initial capitals for main words. For example:

> She collects *The South China Morning Post* on her way to work.
>
> The *Financial Times* devoted its front page to the stock market crash.

Note: Check whether the definite article 'the' is part of the official title. You may omit it if it falls awkwardly as part of the surrounding sentence. For example, either of these is acceptable:

> I expected *The Washington Post* to cover the controversy.
>
> Why didn't today's *Washington Post* have any mention of it?

Magazines and journals

Use italics and initial capitals for main words. For example:

> She renewed her subscriptions to the *National Geographic* and *The Bulletin*.
>
> They have copies of *The New Zealand Medical Journal* and *Woman's Day*.

Films and musicals

Use italics and initial capitals for main words. For example:

> Hoyts Cinemas will screen *Gone with the Wind* and *Mr Bean on Holiday*.
>
> *Phantom of the Opera* is the longest-running show on Broadway, and *The Adventures of Priscilla, Queen of the Desert* opened as a musical at Star City.

Note: French titles use a lesser degree of initial capitals. For example:

> He chose *Monsieur Ibrahim et les fleurs du Coran*, the 2003 film starring Omar Sharif.
>
> The 1972 surrealist film *Le Charme discret de la bourgeoisie* is popular with my students.

Plays and ballets

Use italics and initial capitals for main words. For example:

> Graeme Murphy's 2002 radical reworking of *Swan Lake* was rapturously received.
>
> His favourite plays were Tennessee Williams' *A Streetcar Named Desire* and Alan Bennett's *The History Boys*.

Note: Again, French titles use less initial capitals. For example:

> *Le Ballet comique de la Reine Louise*, a five-hour performance put on in 1581, was a marathon among French court ballets.
>
> Molière collapsed during the fourth performance of *Le Malade imaginaire* and died soon after.

Operas and musical works

Use italics and initial capitals for main words. For example:

> *La Clemenza di Tito* had an all-star cast, and *The Gondoliers* was excellent!
>
> The children opted to listen to their new disc of *Peter and the Wolf* at home.

Note: Musical works with specifically musical titles simply use minimal capitals. For example:

> Chopin's Piano concerto No. 1 in E minor, Op. 1 was playing.
>
> He listened to Brahms' Sonata No. 3 in F minor, Op. 5.

Songs

Titles of individual songs, whether classical or popular, use minimal capitals and quote marks. For example:

> José van Dam, as Leporello, sings the aria 'Notte e giorno faticar' in *Don Giovanni.*
>
> 'The girl from Ipanema' was first recorded commercially in Brazil in 1962.

Radio and television series

Use italics and initial capitals for main words. For example:

> Karl Haas, host of the radio series *Adventures in Good Music*, had a keen sense of humour.
>
> The British TV series *Silent Witness* was first released in 1996, and consisted of two 60-minute parts.

Note: Programs or episodes within series use minimal capitals and quote marks. For example:

> 'Baroque and in debt' was a typically witty program in *Adventures in Good Music.*
>
> 'A guilty mind' is perhaps one of the most disturbing episodes of *Silent Witness.*

Paintings, sculptures and installations

Use italics and minimal capitals. For example:

> Botticelli's *Portrait of a youth* is in the National Gallery of Art in Washington DC.
>
> Klippel's *No. 66 Metal construction* is a finely balanced linear structure in enamel and steel.
>
> The installation by Damien Hirst of carefully arranged seashells, entitled *Forms without life*, expresses perfectly his sentiment that 'you kill things to look at them'.

Technology-related terms

A computer lets you make more mistakes faster than any invention in human history—with the possible exceptions of handguns and tequila.

Anonymous

Our increasing reliance upon technology and the multiple platforms of social media (such as LinkedIn, Facebook, Twitter, Instagram and Pinterest) in both business and personal life has spawned a host of new words and phrases.

Originating within social media, these terms are now migrating into the general lexicon of the English language. In written and spoken form, existing nouns have become verbs (as in 'I'll text him today') and entirely new verbs have been born (as in 'why not google it?').

For example, the following buzzwords are familiar to us all:

> Friend me; I unfriended her.
>
> I tagged you in my post.
>
> It's had over 50 shares.
>
> Look how many likes I've got!
>
> Comment on my status.
>
> I posted it on my timeline (or wall).
>
> Following!
>
> I unfollowed him.
>
> Did you see her latest tweet?

Blogging is my life.

I facebooked him about the event.

It's trending already!

There is also a recurring group of computer-related terms which, when you are writing, should be presented consistently. Here are some of the main ones, listed alphabetically.

Buttons, keys and menus

If referring to specific commands, highlight them or use bold to distinguish them from conventional words italicised for emphasis, and use initial capitals. For example:

Click on the **Log in** button, go to **Tools**, and select **Internet options**.

e-

When 'e' stands for 'electronic', use a hyphen for clarity. For example:

e-banking, e-bay, e-commerce

An exception is 'email' which has entered our vocabulary so fully that it has acquired the status of a single word.

Internet

When referring to 'Internet' in the sense of a proper noun (that is, the global network of communication connecting computers), use an initial capital. When referring to 'internet' adjectivally, or in its abbreviated form 'net', use minimal capitals. For example:

The Internet is a powerful tool.

My internet connection is down so I can't surf the net.

Software and hardware programs

Spell them as they are marketed (usually with initial capitals). Where necessary, include the registered trademark symbol. For example:

> Digital photographers use Adobe® Photoshop, desktop publishers use QuarkXPress, and everyone else uses Windows NT or Apple Macintosh.

Website

Like 'email', this is now universally referred to and rapidly gaining acceptance as a compound word (i.e. 'website' *not* 'web site').

World wide web

This common noun refers to the various servers of the Internet enabling the linking of data. Use minimal capitals, including in its abbreviated form. For example:

> Read that article on the world wide web.
>
> Where would we be without the web?

Note: For details on how to style citations to websites, see 'Bibliographies and references'.

Abbreviations, contractions and acronyms

I am a Bear of Very Little Brain,
and long words Bother me.

AA Milne, Winnie-the-Pooh *(published 1926), Chapter IV*

The modern trend, which would undoubtedly have pleased Pooh Bear, is towards ever more frequent abbreviation, together with minimal capitalisation and sparing use of full stops. This is illustrated in the examples below.

There are subtle differences in the presentation of abbreviations in British English compared with American English. Notably, American English retains the full stops, or periods, to a greater degree than British English, as is also illustrated in the examples below.

Abbreviations (shortened forms of words where the last letter is changed)

In both British English and American English, abbreviated words take full stops at the end. For example:

ch. (i.e. chapter)	Co. (i.e. Company)	cont. (i.e. continued)
no. (i.e. number)	p. (i.e. page)	tel. (i.e. telephone)

Contractions (words that are abbreviated but where the last letter is unchanged)

In British English, words that are contracted take no full stops at the end. For example:

dept (i.e. department)	edn (i.e. edition)	Ltd (i.e. limited)
nos (i.e. numbers)	Rd (i.e. road)	St (i.e. street)

American English is more fluid: while the above usually holds true, contractions may appear with a full stop. Common examples include:

dept. (i.e. department)	Ltd. (i.e. limited)	Rd (i.e. road)

Acronyms (strings of mostly initial letters that are pronounced as words)

Most acronyms are formed from initial letters, some from parts of words, and still others from a blending of initial letters and word parts. In both British and American English, they take no full stops. For example:

NATO (**N**orth Atlantic **T**reaty **O**rganization)	(*initial letters*)
Interpol (**Inter**national Criminal **Pol**ice Organization)	(*parts of words*)
radar (**ra**dio **d**etection **a**nd **r**anging)	(*initial letters and parts of words*)

Note, however, that it is standard American practice to use full stops when referring to the U.S.A. (or U.S.), and to Washington D.C.

Note: Acronyms are sometimes confused with initialisms, which also consist of strings of mostly initial letters. The difference is that initialisms are not pronounced as words. For instance, ATM (automatic teller machine) is an initialism but not an acronym.

Note also that a string of letters can be pronounced as a word in some languages but not in others. For example, IRA is an initialism in English but an acronym in Spanish or Italian.

Academic or professional qualifications

British English increasingly closes up the space between letters within each qualification and omits the full stops. Commas or spaces are used to separate multiple qualifications. For example:

DipEd, GradDip, BA, BSc, MA, PhD

American English also closes up the space between letters, but may retain the full stops. For example:

B.A., M.B.A, Ph.D.

People's titles

As indicated, both British and American English use full stops at the end of abbreviations. For example:

Prof. Silverstein   the Hon. John Miller   Sen. Phelps

At the end of titles, as in other contractions, British English does not use full stops. For example:

Dr Arthur Navarre   Mrs Bernhardt   St Joan of Arc

In American English, contractions may appear with full stops. For example:

Dr. Arthur Navarre Jr.   Mrs. Bernhardt   St. Joan of Arc

People's names

British English closes up the space between capitals and omits full stops. For example:

Hassan M Khalil LT Sanchez PRM Sinclair

American English favours inserting spaces between initials and using full stops. For example:

Hassan M. Khalil L. T. Sanchez P. R. M. Sinclair

Plurals

Most abbreviations in plural form follow the tradition of other English words, with an 's' (without apostrophe) being added at the end. For example:

DVDs PCs TVs

In a few cases the plural is indicated by repeating the first letter and using a full stop. For example:

ll. (i.e. lines) pp. (i.e. pages) ss. (i.e. sections)

Latin abbreviations

In most cases, British English and American English use lower-case roman type with full stops at the end. For example:

c. (*circa*) meaning 'around' or 'about'

et al. (*et alii*) meaning 'and others'

etc. (*et cetera*) meaning 'and so on'

When a Latin usage has become fully anglicised, British English may omit full stops. For example:

am, pm (*ante meridiem, post meridiem*) meaning 'before 12 noon' and 'after 12 noon' respectively e.g. (*exempli gratia*) meaning 'for example' (don't use 'e.g.' and 'etc.' in the same sentence)

i.e. (*id est*) meaning 'that is'

American English, again, favours retaining full stops. For example:

a.m., p.m.

e.g.

i.e.

There are very few Latin abbreviations that use capitals. The most common are:

MS (*manuscriptum*) meaning 'manuscript'

NB (*nota bene*) meaning 'take note'

PS (*postscriptum*) meaning 'postscript'

Numbers

Although he may not always recognize his bondage, modern man lives under a tyranny of numbers.

Nicholas Eberstadt, The Tyranny of Numbers: Mismeasurement and Misrule, *AEI Press, Washington DC, 1995, p. 1*

Should numbers be spelled out or expressed in numerals? Policies vary, depending on house style, specific requirements, and context. For example, in general work with only a few references to numbers, they would probably be spelled out; in highly mathematical or technical material where numbers feature regularly, numerals are more suitable. Follow the house style if there is one; if not, adopt a policy that is natural to your subject matter, is clear and unambiguous, and above all be consistent.

Here is a summary of the most widely accepted conventions.

Numbers below 100

In British English, numbers from one to nine are usually spelled out, and numbers over nine, including fractions, expressed as numerals. Zero is treated as a number. For example:

a total of three items	with a staff of seven
in nine and a half days	about 60 people
with 82 competitors	starting from zero

In American English, numbers below 100, and zero, tend to be spelled out. Fractions are usually expressed as numerals. For example:

a total of three items	with a staff of seven
in 9½ days	about sixty people
with eighty-two competitors	starting from zero

Numbers 100 and upwards

In both British English and American English, numbers over 100 are generally expressed in numerals. For higher or more complex numbers, a combination of words and numerals is often clearer, although if numbers are round, words may be preferable. For example:

at the age of 103	an audience of 2120
an increase of 2.5 million sales	the billion-dollar scheme

Spacing in numbers

The modern tendency is to close up space between numerals that have four digits or less and omit commas, and use a hair space rather than a comma within longer numerals. For example:

4000	40 000	400 000

Spans of numbers

Separate number spans by a closed up en rule (longer than a hyphen but shorter than a dash). Most commonly, minimum digits are used unless a number falls between 11 and 19. For example:

23–8 *not* 23–28 *and not* 23 – 8

13–17 *not* 13–7 *and not* 13 – 7

Note: Exceptions include spans of years, street numbers and roman numerals, all of which are expressed in full. For example:

1993–1996 *or* 1993–96 *not* 1993–6

33–35 Sunset Boulevard *not* 33–5 Sunset Boulevard

xvi–xviii *not* xvi–viii

Starting sentences

Avoid starting a sentence with a numeral (the same applies to headings and captions). Either spell out the numeral or rewrite the sentence. For example:

Eleven people attended the opening *or* the opening was attended by 11 people

not 11 people attended the opening.

Hyphenation

Hyphenate numbers under 100 when they are spelled out. For example:

thirty-four sixty-two ninety-eight

For clarity, avoid strings of hyphenated words, and numerals if necessary. For example:

a five-minute pause *not* a five-minute-pause

a 48-year old man *not* a 48-year-old man *and not* a forty-eight-year-old man

To avoid ambiguity, separate a hyphenated number from other hyphenated words. Regardless of which policy on numbers you're following, the simplest strategy is often to rewrite the sentence. For example:

12 lessons of 30 minutes *not* 12 30-minute lessons

twelve lessons of thirty minutes *not* twelve thirty-minute lessons

Ordinal numbers

When referring to the relative order of numbers (e.g. 'first', 'second') spell out numbers if they are under 100 or if they are large and round. For example:

> the forty-second president *not* the 42nd president
>
> the four-hundredth entry *not* the 400th entry
> (*but* the 402nd entry)

Percentages

British English expresses 'per cent' as two words in generalised material, and uses the '%' symbol in scientific or mathematical contexts. For example:

> He regularly squandered five per cent of his earnings on gambling. (*general*)
>
> Table 2 shows that 18% of patients benefited from the CAT scan. (*medical*)

American English refers to the single word 'percent' in general material, and it is accompanied by numerals rather than words. In specialised contexts, the '%' symbol is considered appropriate. For example:

> He regularly squandered 5 percent of his earnings on gambling. (*general*)
>
> Table 2 shows that 18% of patients benefited from the CAT scan. (*medical*)

Note: In British English, the '%' symbol is used with numerals, whereas the words 'per cent' are used with either numerals or words. For example:

> 8% of passengers *or* eight per cent of passengers
>
> *not* eight % of passengers

Currencies

Place the dollar sign in front of its accompanying number, with no intervening space. The same applies to symbols of other currencies. For example:

US$86 340	C$6782	€5135
R420	NZ$78	A$220

Cents can be shown on their own or as decimal fractions of the dollar. For example:

75c *or* $0.75 *not* $.75

Measurements

Differences between the conventions adopted by Britain and most other English-speaking countries compared to those in America can be confusing.

Britain has adopted the metric system, whereas America uses the Imperial and USA system of measurement. Note the variations between the Imperial and USA systems; for instance, the terms 'hundredweight' and 'ton' (weight) and 'gill' (capacity) have different meanings depending on whether they are Imperial or USA.

Main units of measurement are compared in the table that follows.

Metric system: Length

10 millimetres = 1 centimetre

100 centimetres = 1 metre

1000 metres = 1 kilometre

Metric system: Weight

1000 grams = 1 kilogram

1000 kilograms = 1 ton

Metric system: Capacity

10 millilitres = 1 centilitre

10 centilitres = 1 decilitre

10 decilitres = 1 litre

1000 litres = 1 cubic metre

Imperial/USA system: Length

12 inches = 1 foot

3 feet = 1 yard

5280 feet = 1 mile

Imperial/USA system: Weight

16 ounces = 1 pound (Imperial and USA)

14 pounds = 1 stone (Imperial)

8 stones = 1 hundredweight (112 pounds) (Imperial)

20 hundredweight = 1 ton (2240 pounds) (Imperial)

Imperial system: Capacity

2 teaspoons = 1 dessertspoon

3 teaspoons = 1 tablespoon

2 tablespoons = 1 fluid ounce

5 fluid ounces = 1 gill

2 gills = 1 cup

2 cups = 1 pint (20 fluid ounces

USA system: Capacity

3 teaspoons = 1 tablespoon

2 tablespoons = 1 fluid ounce

4 fluid ounces = 1 gill

2 gills = 1 cup

2 cups = 1 pint (16 fluid ounces)

British English tends to abbreviate units of measurement to a greater extent than does American English, but in both styles there should be a space between a numeral and its unit of measurement. Note that in their abbreviated forms plurals are expressed in same way as the singular, without a final 's'.

In a highly mathematical or technical work, for example, references to units of measurement might read:

28 cm	12 km^2	4 g	200 mL	(*British English*)
11 inches	8 ounces	2 square feet	5 pints	(*American English*)

Roman numerals

These are used for numbering the prelims of a book, some chapter or part numbers, titles of monarchs and popes, and for the Olympic Games. For example:

page viii   Louis XIV   Pope Pius XII   the XXVII Olympiad

Use lower-case roman numerals for page numbering, and capitals for the numbering of chapters or parts. If referring to a span of roman numerals, always express them in full. For example:

page vi–viii   Chapter XV   Part III

Times and dates

… do not squander time, for that is the stuff life is made of.

Benjamin Franklin, American statesman and Founding Father (1706–1790), Poor Richard's Almanack, *June 1746*

British English and American English vary on the presentation of time and dates in some respects, most notably in the sequence of information in dates.

Times of day

Both British and American English spell out the times of day, unless using 'am' or 'pm', or for the sake of precision. For example:

> a one o'clock showing, finishing at three-thirty
>
> an estimated arrival time of six forty-five

Note that British English uses a full stop to separate hours and minutes, whereas American English often uses a colon, and also uses full stops within 'am' and 'pm'. For example:

> departure delayed until 9.32 pm (*British English*)
>
> departure delayed until 9:32 p.m. (*American Engli*sh)

Day–month–year

British English follows a day–month–year sequence, whereas American English follows a month–day–year sequence. In both styles, this applies when dates are spelled out or expressed numerically. For example:

16 October 1989 *or* 16.10.89 (*British English*)

October 16,1989 *or* 10.16.89 (*American English*)

To avoid the obvious risks of ambiguity between the two approaches, spell out the month where possible. For simplicity, omit suffixes such as 'th' or 'st', superscript or otherwise, after days.

Decades and centuries

Use numerals to express decades, and omit apostrophes. For example:

the 1790s *not* the seventeen-nineties

the 1920s *not* the twenties, the 1920's, the '20s

Space permitting, spell out the names of centuries. For example:

the twelfth century *not* the 12th century *and not* the 12C

twelfth-century beliefs *not* 12th century beliefs *and not* 12C beliefs

BC/AD and BCE/CE

Ensure that there is a space between the year and 'BC' (before Christ) or 'AD' (*anno Domini*), or between the year and 'BCE' (before the common era) or 'CE' (the common era). Note that the year precedes the era. For example:

44 BC *not* 44BC *and not* BC44

12 BCE *not* 12BCE *and not* BCE12

Use full numerals for date spans. For example:

220–245 AD *not* 200–45 AD

370–380 CE *not* 370–80 CE

Plurals

With dates, as elsewhere, indicate the plural form by adding the letter 's', and only use an apostrophe beforehand if expressing plurals of single numbers (or letters). For example:

> by the 1940s *not* by the 1940's
>
> counting by 4's *not* counting by 4s

Starting a sentence

Spell out a date or time when it occurs at the beginning of a sentence, rewriting the sentence if necessary. This applies both when, as in British English, the day precedes the month, as well as in American English when the month appears first. For example:

> His birthday is 27 May 1997 *not* 27 May 1997 is his birthday. (*British English)*
>
> His birthday is May 27, 1997 *not* May 27, 1997 is his birthday. (*American English*)
>
> Twelve o'clock is too late! *not* 12 o'clock is too late! (*British and American English*)

Lists

There is something at once uplifting and terrifying about the idea that nothing in the world is so unique that it can't be entered on a list.

Attributed to Georges Perec, French writer and film-maker (1936–82)

Lists can be a useful device for signposting information, as long as they are not overused which can disrupt the flow of the text. They should be internally coherent, based on a consistent grammatical structure and pattern of punctuation, and ideally displayed with a space above and below.

Most lists are numbered or bulleted.

Numbered lists

Use for items that take a particular sequence or ranking, or where the list is exhaustive. Numbers that exceed nine are aligned on the right (except roman numerals which are aligned on the left). Use bold for numbers and omit full stops. Use lower-case letters for a second order of items, and roman numerals for a third order.

For example:

The professor argued that the primary causes of the French Revolution could be broken down to three:

1 The *Ancien Régime*, the existing system of government, which

- **a** centralised power, exemplified in
  - i the nature of the Court of Versailles
  - ii the *lettre de cachet* which effectively crushed all dissent
- **b** rewarded the nobles and clergy, whose privileges included
  - i exorbitant salaries and ownership of land
  - ii exemption from taxation
- **c** punished the peasants with
  - i heavy taxation
  - ii enforced military service and labour on public services
  - iii frequent imprisonments, torture and executions
- **d** fuelled the grievances of the bourgeoisie, who were
  - i not allowed to have a share in government
  - ii excluded from important official posts in the army, navy and diplomatic service
  - iii resentful at the lack of religious freedom.

2 The influence of the philosophers, and in particular

- **a** Voltaire, with his
  - i relentless political satire of institutions—*Candide*
  - ii insistence on fighting miscarriages of justice
- **b** Montesquieu, with his
  - i model for democracy—*De l'Esprit des Lois*
  - ii influence on revolutionary leaders
- **c** Rousseau, who ignited the spirit of revolt with speeches on
  - i Liberty, Equality and the Sovereignty of the People
  - ii an alternative government—*Du Contrat Social.*

3 Involvement in the American War of Independence, which led to
   a American democratic ideas spreading with the soldiers' return
   b further massive costs to France's already-buckling treasury.

Bulleted lists

Use for shorter items, or for those that have no particular sequence. Use en rules for subdivisions, and indent any turnover lines.

For example:

> She listened to the professor's lecture, but objected that equally important in bringing about the revolution were:
> - the long-term extravagance of previous monarchies
>   – Louis XIV, the Sun King
>   – Louis XV
> - the personalities of Louis XIV and Marie Antionette
>   – indecisiveness of the king
>   – political naivety of the queen
> - the famine of the winter of 1789
>   – harvests ruined, raising price of corn and causing widespread starvation
>   – a mob of desperate peasants converging on Paris.

Punctuating lists

To avoid confusion, adopt a single policy and apply it consistently. The following policy is simple, clear and allows for grammatical flexibility.

Introduce each list with a colon in order to link it with the preceding text from which it flows. Although not essential for longer or numbered lists, grammar dictates that it nearly always is with shorter lists, as in the example above.

Where listed items form discrete sentences within themselves (this can take the form of questions), each item should begin with a capital letter and end with a full stop (or question mark), as in the example that follows.

> Two sentences in the diary made a deep impression on the child:
>
> 1 Marie Antoinette's last words were '*Pardonnez-moi monsieur*', after she had accidentally stepped on the executioner's foot.
>
> 2 With shorn hair and hands bound, she walked up to the guillotine with dignity and courage, and the crowd fell silent.

Where listed items form incomplete sentences, observe minimal punctuation. Each item should start with a lower-case letter and have no punctuation except the full stop after the last item, as in the example that follows.

> The eye-witness maintained in his diary that the queen:
>
> - apologised to her executioner when she stepped on his foot
> - displayed dignity and courage in her final moments.

Illustrations

A picture shows me at a glance what it takes ten pages of text to describe.

Ivan Turgenev, Fathers and Sons *(published 1861), Chapter XVI*

In addition to traditional drawings and sketches, the term 'illustration' covers cartoons, line diagrams and maps, and black-and-white photos (often loosely referred to as halftones).

Illustrations do not suit all writing, and should not be used as mere fillers. If you feel that your manuscript would be improved by some illustration, you can either brief an artist to create them or provide them yourself.

Briefing an artist

Jot down your ideas and a brief description of what you would like at the appropriate place in the manuscript (e.g. 'p. 4: Insert black-and-white photo of typical suburban family relaxing in garden, Sydney, 1950s'). Better still, prepare a simple sketch (called a 'rough') to suggest what you have in mind. You don't have to create perfect, finished artwork, but you do need to communicate clearly what you envisage so that the artist can create it. If possible, provide a reference to (or photocopy of) another similar illustration upon which yours could be styled.

If your manuscript is accepted for publication, an editor will work with you to have the illustrations created, and also to size them and decide whether to present them portrait (vertically) or landscape (horizontally). If you decide to commission your own artwork independently from an artist or graphic design company, your primary role remains to specify and communicate your intentions. Many a manuscript has been enhanced by illustrations created *after* the writing is completed.

Providing your own illustrations

Although you do not have to provide your own illustrations, if you can do so it is clearly an advantage. If so, allow a space in the text and place each illustration precisely where you wish it to appear with its caption beneath. Alternatively, you can gather all the illustrations together at the end of the manuscript, insert instructions (on separate lines) at the relevant places in the text (e.g. 'p. 37: Insert pic 1.2'), and provide a separate list of captions (called 'caption copy').

Sourcing existing illustrations

If you wish to reproduce an illustration from an existing publication, you must first clear permission (the earlier the better, in case permission is refused and you're obliged to research an alternative illustration). Refer to the Appendix for a permissions letter template that you can copy and tailor to your individual needs.

Once permission is granted and any conditions met, a formal acknowledgment should be made. (In the case of books this includes author, year of publication, title, publisher, place of publication, and page number.) You can do this either in a single credit line beneath the picture itself or, in highly illustrated material where there are multiple credits, gathered as part of separate list of acknowledgments with an expression of gratitude, if appropriate. For example:

Source: *The Guardian*, 17 November 2008, p. 10

Reproduced by kind permission of the Obolensky family collection (*single credit*)

For illustrative matter, the following sources are gratefully acknowledged: *The New Zealand Herald*, 6 March 2003 for the photographs on pp. 24 and 58; Fotopress for the plates on pp. 79, 198 and 233; …

Photo credits: Alexander Turnbull Library for Plates 2 and 17; Getty Images Gallery for the back cover picture and Plates 23 and 36; … (*multiple credits*)

Numbering

Number all illustrations consecutively by chapter, like this: Figure 3.1, 3.2, 3.3 and so forth (i.e. Chapter 3, Figure 1; Chapter 3, Figure 2 and so on). The term 'figure' covers all types of illustrations as well as typographical displays such as tables. Place captions after the figure numbers. This is universal practice, and allows you to add to or remove figures at any time without renumbering all subsequent ones or adjusting cross-references—an exercise both time-consuming and prone to error.

Photographs

If you're providing photos, they must be of a high quality (i.e. high resolution). Black-and-white photos, being cheaper to reproduce, are often a more practical option than colour. Ideally, photos can be supplied as JPEG files, but if you supply hard copy photos, keep them carefully in a separate folder and do not fold them, cut them or use paperclips on them. Rather than writing directly onto the back of a photo, write your instruction on a separate label and attach it to the reverse.

Cropping and framing

Remember that selecting a portion of the whole is a smart way to improve the overall effect of an illustration, and costs nothing. If you wish to cut away part of an illustration (referred to as 'cropping'), indicate the 'crop marks' on a photocopy, not on the original. Try placing your key feature at the intersections of thirds. An object in the centre does not elicit the viewer's interest; placed even slightly off-centre, it encourages the eye to move around the whole area.

Preparing an artwork brief

Whether or not you're able to provide your own illustrations, it is helpful to create a separate document, known as an 'artwork brief', that summarises what is needed, and where. This is an easy way to keep track of your own ideas, as well as making it easy for anyone else looking through your manuscript to grasp them immediately.

A typical artwork brief might begin like this:

Artwork #	Ms page #	Size	Description	Notes/source
1.1	7	5 x 7 cm	Cartoon: 2 boys and 3 girls playing	To create—make sure girl is prominent
1.2	19	½ page	Diagram: cross-section of house	Labels and arrow needed (see rough)
1.3	34	Full page	Map: Flamingo Bay, showing Connell Rd	Highlight Connell Rd (see ph/copy p. 9, *City Streets*)

Note: Refer to the Appendix for an artwork brief template that you can copy and tailor to your individual needs.

Tables, charts and graphs

If you have more than two related numbers, consider presenting them in a table, chart or graph. Numbers almost always work better in one of these formats than in prose …

S Buttry, 'Telling a story in a multimedia world', article in No Train No Gain, former training website for journalists, archives viewed 25 February 2018

Tables consist of purely typographical matter; charts include flow charts, bar charts and pie charts; and graphs can be line, dot or illustrated. The primary purpose of all three is to illustrate what is explained in the text and to expand on established themes. As such, they are valuable devices for showing trends or overall patterns.

If you use displays, make sure that there is a good balance between the quantity of displays and amount of textual explanation. A few tables, charts or graphs are effective; very many are less so and can interrupt the rhythm of the text. Display data only if by doing so you're able to make a point more succinctly and clearly than by textual explanation, and keep displays as brief and simple as possible.

It is probably easiest to position each table, chart or graph precisely where you want it in the course of writing your manuscript. If, however, you have many to create (in, say, an economics book), you may find it helpful to provide them separately, complete with headings and captions, and insert instructions, each on a separate line, at the relevant places in the text (e.g. 'Insert Table 4.5').

Numbering

Number all tables, charts and graphs consecutively by chapter, like this: Table 1.1, 1.2, Chart 2.1 (i.e. Chapter 1, Table 1; Chapter 1, Table 2, Chapter 2, Table 1).

Headings and captions

A one-line heading, or title, per table, chart or graph is usually ideal—it beckons to readers where a longer heading may lose their attention. More detailed information can be included in a caption, positioned beneath the display.

Design

Avoid excessively small type sizes, and columns or rows placed close together, both of which reduce readability, especially in tables. If highly detailed and lengthy displays are necessary, it may help to position them landscape (i.e. horizontally) on pages by themselves.

Sourcing existing tables, charts and graphs

If you wish to reproduce a table, chart or graph from an existing publication, you must first clear permission and include a full credit beneath the display.

The style of credit lines varies slightly depending on house style. Most are based on the author–date system, but note that the author's initials precede the surname, and the year of publication goes at the end, as in these examples:

> *Source*: Based on statistics in JP Przybylski, *Agricultural Policy and Performance in Poland*, Routledge and K Paul, London, 2014, chapter 3, pp. 89–115

Source: Independent survey reproduced in GL Cavendish, *The Future of Unions*, Pergamon Press, Sydney, 1991, p. 46

Source: Hunter Financial Group Ltd, Annual super statement, 30 May 2009

Bibliographies and references

The word 'bibliography' comes from the two Greek words *biblion*, meaning 'book', and *graphein*, meaning 'to write'. It was first used by the ancient Greeks to signify the copying of books by hand ...

Today, 'bibliography' refers to the study of books as physical objects, and also to the list of works at the end of a book—in the sense used here. The works included in a bibliography may be cited in the text, used as source materials in the creation of the text, or simply considered by the author to be pertinent to the subject. The purpose of a bibliography is to supply a general context of relevant material for interested readers to deepen their knowledge of the subject.

A reference list is more specific than a bibliography, and includes only those works cited in the text (that is, quoted from or referred to). The purpose of a reference list is to furnish the reader with sufficient information to find each work.

There are various styles of presenting bibliographies and reference lists, and they are determined as much by subject matter as by house style. Most styles are based on the 'author–date system' in which the author's name is followed by the year of publication—although there are many fine variations between one style and another, particularly in terms of capitalisation (initial capitals for titles or not?), punctuation (comma or full stop to separate elements?) and the use of brackets to enclose publishing information (place of publication and year, or just year?). Once you have established which style is appropriate to your material, the cardinal rule is, as often, internal consistency.

The most common styles applied internationally to citations include:

- Harvard style, or 'author–date system' (developed by a professor at Harvard University)—lists titles in alphabetical order by author's name, followed by the year of publication; suits a wide range of subject matters and forms the basis of most other styles
- Chicago style (detailed in *The Chicago Manual of Style*)—one of the most widely used styles for general works, especially in the humanities
- APA style (style of the American Psychological Association)—also popular, especially in the area of social and behavioural sciences; includes formatting specifications
- AMA (style of the American Medical Association)—used for scholarly works in medical science and related areas
- MLA (style of the Modern Language Association of America)—used for academic works to do with language and literature, especially in America and Canada
- Cambridge style—advanced by the University of Cambridge Press and used widely in the UK, particularly in the area of social science.

The following sample titles illustrate the 'author–date system'. Based on the *Style Manual for Authors, Editors and Printers* in Australia, they deviate in minor points of style from the conventions outlined above, yet offer a clear general pattern of referencing according to the author–date system.

Books

1. Author's or editor's family name followed by a comma and the initial/s with no punctuation afterwards.
2. Year of publication followed by a comma.
3. Title of publication, in italics, followed by a comma.
4. Edition (if appropriate) followed by a comma.
5. Publisher followed by a comma.
6. Place of publication followed by a stop if final or by a comma if a page reference follows.
7. Page number/s (if appropriate) followed by a full stop.

For example:

> Freeman, M 2008 (ed.), *Domestic Violence*, Ashgate Publishing, Aldershot, pp. 224–9.
>
> Klein, N 2015, *This Changes Everything: Capitalism vs. the Climate*, Penguin Books Ltd, London, p. 89.

Chapters in books

1. Author's (i.e. contributor's) family name followed by a comma and the initial/s with no punctuation afterwards.
2. Year of publication followed by a comma.
3. Chapter title enclosed in single quote marks, using minimal capitals, and followed by a comma and the word 'in'.
4. Author's or editor's initial/s and family name followed by a comma.
5. Title of publication, in italics, followed by a comma.
6. Edition (if applicable) followed by a comma.

7. Publisher followed by a comma.
8. Place of publication followed by a stop if final or by a comma if a page reference follows.
9. Inclusive page numbers of chapter followed by a full stop.

For example:

> Mehta, SP 1998, 'Complementary leadership', in P Chang, T Sendut & A Halili (eds), *Understanding Asian Management*, 3rd edn, Allen & Unwin, Sydney, pp. 125–66.
>
> Schmidt, R 2001, 'Genetics, inheritance and variation', in E Locke, *Physiology of the Human Body*, WB Saunders, Philadelphia, pp. 35–58.

Articles in journals and magazines

1. Author's family name followed by a comma and the initial/s with no punctuation afterwards.
2. Year of publication followed by a comma.
3. Title of article enclosed in single quote marks, using minimal capitals, followed by a comma.
4. Title of periodical, in italics, followed by a comma. (Note that the place of publication is usually omitted.)
5. Volume number and, if appropriate, issue number enclosed in brackets, followed by a comma.
6. Date of publication followed by a comma.
7. Page number/s followed by a full stop.

For example:

> Bloch, S 2004, 'A pioneer in psychotherapy research: Aaron Beck', *Australian and New Zealand Journal of Psychiatry*, vol. 38(11–12), Nov.–Dec., pp. 55–86.

Denby, D 1998, 'The contender: Have we been missing the point about Norman Mailer?', *The New Yorker*, 20 Apr., p. 60.

Newspaper articles

1. Author's family name followed by a comma and the initial/s with no punctuation afterwards.
2. Year of publication followed by a comma.
3. Title of article enclosed in single quote marks, using minimal capitals, followed by a comma.
4. Name of newspaper, in italics, followed by a comma.
5. Date of publication followed by a comma.
6. Page number/s, if applicable, followed by a full stop.

For example:

Armitage, T 2007, 'Switzerland urged to pardon Anna Göldi, Europe's last witch', *The Independent*, 2 Aug., p. 11.

Wells, J 2011, 'Black wields a poison pen in jailhouse memoir', *Toronto Star*, 1 Sept., p. 1.

Unpublished works (e.g. conference papers or theses)

1. Author's family name followed by a comma and the initial/s with no punctuation afterwards.
2. Year of release followed by a comma.
3. Title of work enclosed in single quote marks, using minimal capitals, followed by a comma.
4. Academic qualification if applicable, followed by a comma.
5. Name of associated university or other educational institution followed by a full comma.

6. Place of release (if not already clear from preceding information) followed by a comma.
7. Date of release if available, followed by a full stop.

For example:

Boamah, S 2003, 'Towards sustainable housing provision in Queensland rural and remote Aboriginal communities', PhD thesis, University of Queensland.

Jordan, K 1998, 'Prevalence and characteristics of pediatric Chronic Fatigue Syndrome', paper presented at the Bi-annual Research Conference of the American Association for Chronic Fatigue Syndrome, Cambridge, Massachusetts, 10–11 Oct.

Websites

1. Author or authoring body followed by a comma.
2. Title of document, in italics, followed by a comma.
3. Date the document was viewed.
4. URL address enclosed in angle brackets followed by a stop.

For example:

The Sydney Morning Herald, 'The petro is born': Venezuela launches its cryptocurrency, viewed 21 Feb. 2018 <http://www.smh.com.au/world/the-petro-is-born-venezuela-launches-its-cryptocurrency-20180220-h0we33.html>.

MIT, *Technology Review, Stem-cell engineering offers a lifeline to endangered species,* viewed 4 Sept. 2011 <http://www.technologyreview.com/biomedicine/38510/?ref=rss>.

In-text citations, footnotes and endnotes

Having to look up from the text and go down to a footnote is like being interrupted while making love to go downstairs and answer the door.

Noel Coward, quoted in A Grafton, The Footnote: A Curious History, *Cambridge, Harvard University Press, 1997, p. 70*

The earliest footnotes probably appeared in the twelfth century. They became more sophisticated during the Renaissance when the discovery of important texts led to a surge in cross-referencing and annotation. By the eighteenth and nineteenth century, annotation was virtually considered an art form in its own right (writers such as Coleridge, Fielding and Pope famously used footnotes for satire as well as serious commentary).

Coward's witticism bears testament to a more modern frustration with various forms of annotation. They seem to intrude on the central theme and require us to put one train of thought on hold while we examine another; they annoy us and we want to skip them. Perhaps fortunately, the majority of works require no annotation. In other texts, scholarly or otherwise, annotation is an essential tool for referencing and commentary as long as we don't fall into the trap of offering the reader 'only a thin and fragile crust of text on which to cross the deep, dark swamp of commentary' (as Grafton said of the seventeenth-century French philosopher, Pierre Bayle, in whose dictionary even the footnotes had footnotes).

There are three forms of annotation: in-text citations, footnotes and endnotes. Although there are slight variances in their presentation, most annotations follow the style of the examples below. As is the case with all referencing, consistency in presentation is crucial.

In-text citations

These are brief references to other texts, the details of which the reader can follow up separately. In-text citations generally follow the 'author–date system'; that is, they appear within brackets, preferably at the end of the sentence, and in the following order:

1. Author's or editor's surname with no punctuation afterwards.
2. Year of publication followed by a colon (or a comma and 'p.' or 'pp.').
3. Page number/s followed by a full stop (outside the final bracket if the reference refers only to the preceding sentence).

For example:

> For lack of evidence and from the eventual failure of Akhenaten's ideas to survive his death, it is easy to conclude that the cult of the Aten had little popular following (Kemp 1989: 301).

To refer to multiple authors, use a semicolon to separate references. For example:

> Old Kingdom documents refer to the existence of 'pyramid towns' looked after by a hierarchy of officials, proving that organised life at pyramid sites did not end with the burial of the king (Helck 1957: 91–111; Kitchen 1973: 103–9).

Footnotes

These are notes placed at the foot of individual pages, set in a smaller type size than the main text, and linked to it by means of superscript, or raised, numerals placed after the final punctuation.

Notes are numbered consecutively, with each chapter starting from one. Most programs, like Microsoft Word, automatically number footnotes. In lieu of such a program, it is important to be careful with inserting footnotes: changes to all but the last mean that subsequent numerals must be altered, which is frustrating, time-consuming and increases the margin for error.

Footnotes are less popular than endnotes, largely because they are more intrusive. If you choose to use them, keep them as succinct as possible.

The purpose of footnotes is to supply the source of information, to offer a commentary or varying opinions on the subject, or to give evidence or examples that are too lengthy or not sufficiently relevant to incorporate in the body of the text. For example:

> Both Heyerdahl and von Däniken brushed aside overwhelming evidence that the Easter Islanders were typical Polynesians derived from Asia rather than from the Americas, and that their culture (including even their statues) also grew out of Polynesian culture.[1]

The superscript '1' links in with the note at the bottom of the page. References are usually set out as below (similar to the author–date system except that the author's initials precede the surname, and the year of publication goes at the end). For example:

> [1] JM Diamond, *Collapse: How Societies Choose to Fail or Succeed*, Viking, New York, 2005, p. 86.

Endnotes

These are a list of notes collected either at the end of each chapter, or more properly at the end of the book. Like footnotes, they are set in a smaller type size than the main text, and linked to it by means of superscript numerals placed after the final punctuation.

Notes are numbered consecutively, with each chapter starting from one. Again, ensure that numerals are correct to avoid any renumbering. (Symbols are usually reserved for mathematical works to avoid confusion between superscript numerals and indexes.)

Like footnotes, the purpose of endnotes is to allow you to supply the source of information and offer commentary or elaboration on a subject. There is usually plenty of space available at the end of a chapter (or book), so endnotes tend to be more discursive than footnotes. For example:

> The general perception was that Holt was nice to the point that his 'essential decency was viewed as weakness', whereas Gorton gave the impression of being 'prepared to be rough, tough and nasty' if the situation required it.[2]

The superscript '2' links in with a '2' in the endnotes for the appropriate chapter. References are set out as follows (similar to the author–date system except that the author's initials precede the surname, and the year of publication goes at the end). For example:

> [2] For a detailed interpretation of the differing leadership styles of Prime Ministers Holt and Gorton, see A Reid, *The Power Struggle*, Shakespeare Head Press, Sydney, 1969, p. 13.

Referencing shortcuts

Within footnotes and endnotes there are various shorthand methods for referring to previously cited works. The most common are listed below.

et al.

To refer to an already cited work with three or more authors, use the first author's surname followed by 'et al.' (short for the Latin *et alii*, meaning 'and others'). For example:

> Miller, JW, Levinsky, S, Hartog, AT & Selwyn, PG 1989, *The History of Calligraphy*, Routledge, London.

can subsequently be referred to as

> Miller et al.

ibid.

To refer to a work identical to that cited immediately above, use 'ibid.' (short for the Latin *ibidem*, meaning 'in the same place'). For example:

> Grunwald, L 2011, *The Irresistible Henry House*, Random House, New York.
>
> ibid.

and to include a page reference

> ibid., p. 175.

op. cit.

To refer to an already cited work, but to a different page, use 'op. cit.' (short for the Latin *opere citato* meaning 'in work cited'). For example:

> Boran, P 2010, *The Invisible Prison: Scenes from an Irish Childhood*, Dedalus Press, Dublin, p. 28.

would be referred to later as

> Boran op. cit., p. 51.

loc. cit.

To refer to the same page of an already cited work, use 'loc. cit.' (short for the Latin *loco citato* meaning 'in place cited'). For example:

> Boran loc. cit.

Indexes

A good index is a work of art and science, order and chance, delight and usefulness.

AS Byatt, in her foreword to Hazel K Bell (ed.) Indexers and Indexes in Fact and Fiction, *British Library, London, 2001*

The purpose of a general index is to enable the reader to locate a subject or theme. Specialised indexes are less common, but typically cover names of people and places. If a work is very short an index may not be necessary, particularly if the contents list is comprehensive and gives a breakdown of the various components. With a lengthier work an index will probably be necessary or desirable; a good one lends a book credibility, as well as being a strong selling point.

The language and length of an index depends on the nature of the material and on its intended readership. Clearly, an index in a book on forensic medicine will be pitched at a different level from that in a general book on home decoration.

An index should be as concise as possible. An excessively long index discourages the reader from using it, and as it is set in a smaller type size than the rest of the text it can, to some, present a visual challenge.

Be they specialised or general, all indexes rely on an ability on the part of the indexer to be analytical and to isolate key events, people and places, as well as being sensitive to themes and topics. This holds true regardless of what indexing package is used.

The index is best started after the manuscript is complete, ideally at page proof stage when it is certain that no more changes will be introduced and page numbers are final. It is possible to begin an index without having final page numbers, but obviously they will have to be dropped in later, which is a fiddly process.

If, in the course of writing, you wish to note down entries that will ultimately be included in an index, you can run off a spare copy of your manuscript and use it to highlight the main entries. Sub-entries can be identified in a different highlighter.

Compiling a general index

Although the presentation of indexes may vary according to house style, here are some basic rules that can be observed when compiling a general index:

- List all main headings and subheadings in alphabetical order. Treat hyphenated words as single words unless otherwise identical (e.g. 'rebate' precedes 're-entry', and 're-cover' precedes 'recover').
- Main headings include major subjects and names and, depending on the readership, themes.
- Use lower-case letters throughout, unless it would contradict convention (e.g. proper names retain initial capitals).
- Use commas after headings and to separate page references.
- Use a regular type size and one column per page for ease of compilation (the type size can be reduced later, at the same time as the design is finalised, including the number of columns).
- Introduce an extra line space, or half a line space, to separate the 'a' entries from the 'b' entries, and so on.

- Indent subheadings, and use a double indent for sub-subheadings (but note that the latter can be confusing and are best avoided).
- Indent any lines of entries that run over (known as 'turnover lines') more than the smallest subheading. That is, if there is one level of subheading, indent turnover lines twice; if there are two levels of subheading (i.e. sub-subheadings), indent turnover lines three times.
- Use minimal numbers in number spans (e.g. 41–3 *not* 41–43) except when the result may be confusing; that is, when listing numbers 11–19 (e.g. 311–14 *not* 311–4 *and not* 311–314).
- To cross-reference, use *see* and *see also* at the end of the main heading, irrespective of alphabetical order.
- When a heading is a major theme referred to over many pages, though not on all, use *passim* (Latin for 'in many places').

Compiling a name index

Here are some points to bear in mind when compiling a name index:

- Close up two or more initials, and omit full stops.
- (e.g. JP Salieri *not* J. P. Salieri or J P Salieri).
- Spell out the author's first name if this is its most recognisable form or to avoid ambiguity (e.g. Leonardo da Vinci *not* da Vinci, L).
- Alphabetise names with initial articles and prepositions according to how they usually appear (e.g. d'Amico, de la Paz, van Gogh).

- Treat both 'Mc' and 'Mac' as 'Mac' (e.g. 'McCartney' would precede 'MacDonald'), and treat both 'St' and 'Saint' as 'Saint' (e.g. 'St Aloysius' College' would precede 'Saint Ignatius').

Here is an example of a typical index which contains examples of the above:

P

parent's attitudes, 11–14
peer relationships, *see* relationships
persona dolls, 64
anti-bias research project, 168–80, 96, 112
physical development, 12–21
Piaget, J, 60–2, 69–70
  developmental theory, 61, 69, 76
  responsibility, 64, 88
  play categories, 32, 41
  see also genetic epistemology
play, 11–18, 32–7, 89–91
  categories, 32–6
  constructivist perspective, 13–17
  opportunities for gifted children, 89
pretend play, *see* dramatic play
projective play, 31–34

R

racial awareness, 167
racial bias, 169
racism, 172–89 *passim*
relationships 79
  peer, 9–12
  understanding, 11
representational play, 51
risk in play, 84, 90, 97
  see also gender boundaries
risk-taking, 65–8
role play, 16, 22–3, 44, 65,
  cultural characteristics
    African, 73, 75
    Asian, 27–9
    European, 44, 49

Hiring an indexer

If you do not feel confident or lack the time to compile your own index you can, depending on your budget, consider hiring a professional indexer. Indexing involves far more than listing keywords; it is an intellectual activity that involves analysing a book and identifying those terms and concepts that readers would search for.

Begin by researching your national society of professional indexers to narrow down those who are versed in your subject area, and available. It's a good idea to ask for a list of books they have indexed, or a sample of their recent work. You can also check their testimonials in their website.

Find out whether they charge by the hour or have a fixed fee, and establish the cost of the index. For what constitutes a 'reasonable' hourly rate, contact your society of indexers.

Once you have found a suitable indexer and agreed a price and timeframe, prepare a clear written brief.

Here are some basic guidelines to follow when briefing your indexer:

- Explain the nature of index you would like (e.g. a general index or a name index?) and indicate its ideal length and level of detail (e.g. how many levels, if any, of subentry?)
- Compile a list of the type of index items you wish to be included from your first chapter or two—this will help clarify your own expectations.
- Explain the intended readership, and define the level of linguistic complexity which would be appropriate for the index (e.g. do you want to distinguish references to illustrations from general page references?)
- If possible, provide a photocopy of another index that can be followed for style (several pages will do).

Finally, check the finished index carefully against your original brief. An obvious strategy is to select various key words and verify that they are included. If any part of your brief has not been followed, and no clarification requested, you're entitled to ask that it be revised (which underlines the importance of a clear, thorough brief in the first place).

PART THREE:
Publishing Options

Author's checklist

'Just one more thing ...'

Lieutenant Columbo, detective with the LAPD, American TV series, 1970s

Columbo's catchcry applies to many a writer struggling to bring a manuscript to conclusion. Authors traditionally share the detective's reluctance to 'let go' of a situation. It can be extremely difficult to sign off on a manuscript you've been working on for some time, and say, once and for all, 'I've finished!'

To finalise your manuscript, ask yourself:

- Is there any outstanding copy?
- Are there any unresolved queries?
- Are all pages numbered? (remember to use roman numerals for the prelims, and arabic numerals for the main body of the text)
- Are the prelims prepared, including any foreword, contents, preface or acknowledgments?
- Are any illustrations or roughs prepared? (keyed in to the text or gathered separately)
- Are any captions to illustrations supplied?
- Are tables, charts or graphs supplied? (keyed in to the text or gathered separately)

- Are captions or labels to tables, charts or graphs drawn up?
- Are quotes fully sourced?
- Is copyright cleared on all longer/substantive quotes?
- Is copyright cleared on any tables, charts or graphs where necessary?
- Has due acknowledgment been made for all copyright material used?
- Is the appendix, glossary or reference section, if appropriate, prepared?
- Is the bibliography complete and presented consistently?
- Have the entries for an index, if you're using one, been prepared?
- Have you backed up your whole manuscript?

When you can tick off all these questions, you're ready to publish!

If you wish to submit your manuscript to traditional publishing companies, read on.

If you wish to self-publish, skip straight to the chapter on self-publishing or independent publishing.

Traditional publishing

'It is impossible to sell animal stories in the USA.'

The editor at Dial Press, New York,
rejecting Animal Farm, *1944*

After the manuscript had been turned down by all the main publishing houses in the UK, it was published by Secker & Warburg in 1945. It became an instant bestseller.

A traditional or commercial publisher, which can consist of an individual, a partnership, a group or a company, takes on the financial responsibility of producing and publishing a book it believes is worthwhile and will sell. A reputable publishing house will exchange a standard publishing contract with you and pay for the editing of your manuscript, its internal page design and cover artwork. It organises printing and distribution of your book to retail outlets, as well as marketing—though it increasingly expects you, as author, to do your share of publicity (e.g. participate in talks and engage actively in promotion on social media). You receive author's royalties on all sales.

The snag is that only a small percentage of unsolicited manuscripts are accepted for publication. This is not only due to the nature and quality of a manuscript, but also because book publishing is run on a tight budget and most publishers are genre-driven; that is, they are obliged to focus on subjects that fall strictly within pre-established categories. (The term 'genre' is usually applied to fiction, and 'category' to nonfiction.)

For example, you may have written a book inspiring people to overcome their hurdles and find peace, but if a company does not publish inspirational or New Age literature there is no point sending it your proposal. Even if the company agrees to look at your proposal, there is no guarantee that it will be interested in publishing it.

So, it pays to do your research on publishing houses and their areas of speciality. Start by drawing up a list of local publishing houses and find out what material each requires. In addition to a synopsis and sample chapters, companies typically request a contents list, a synopsis, an author bio, an assessment of the audience, and a description of similar or competing titles showing how the manuscript fills a gap in the market.

It is best to place your material with one publisher at a time, so that each one has sole right of inspection and you can easily keep track of it.

Electronic submissions are the norm, but if you're posting your material, send a clear photocopy using recorded delivery and enclosing a SASE (i.e. a self-addressed, stamped envelope). If a publisher is local, you may choose to offer to drop it off and collect it later.

Finally, whether emailing or posting your submissions, always keep your originals intact lest they are lost or not returned.

Literary agents

If your overtures to publishing houses are rejected, you may wish to enlist the support of a literary agent. Literary agents work on your behalf to try and place your manuscript with a publisher and ensure that your rights as author are fully respected. Their commission on sales generated is approximately 15 per cent.

First, make sure that you select a reputable agent. Your local literary agents' association is a good starting point, although the accuracy of the information contained usually relies on the honesty of the agents themselves. Note that legitimate agents should *not* ask for an upfront fee for simply assessing your manuscript (in some countries, agents who demand upfront fees are disqualified from membership of literary agents' associations).

Second, finding a good literary agent is fast becoming almost as hard as finding a publisher. Many agents, like publishing houses, do not accept unsolicited manuscripts or manuscripts by previously unpublished authors. Even if one does agree to represent your manuscript, this is no guarantee of publication.

Nevertheless, finding an agent can be an important first step towards publication. With in-depth knowledge of what companies are looking for, and an array of personal and professional contacts, a literary agent is in a unique position to give you feedback and assist you.

Start by compiling a list of available agents, local ones first, and narrow it down to those who invite submissions from the genre or category into which your manuscript fits. Then contact each one and, as with publishers, confirm that they are interested to see your manuscript proposal and what information they require.

Place your material with one agent at a time. Electronic submission is simplest, but if you post it, use recorded delivery and enclose a SASE.

Finally, as with commercial publishers, always back up your work or retain the original in case yours is lost or not returned.

Manuscript assessment services

If the feedback you receive from literary agents suggests that your manuscript needs rewriting, you may consider having your manuscript assessed professionally.

Manuscript assessment services are run by professionals who, for a fee, provide independent, detailed appraisals of manuscripts including their strengths and weaknesses, and make suggestions for improvement. If you decide to take this step, bear in mind two points.

First, make sure that you're motivated by a desire to improve your writing rather than to impress publishers or agents, both of whom prefer to make their own assessment of a manuscript's marketability rather than rely on someone else's.

Second, as with literary agents, be wary when selecting an assessor for your manuscript. Check people's credentials and ensure that they are listed with your local literary agency or society of authors.

Writing a synopsis

Although the nature of your synopsis depends on your material, the purpose of all synopses is identical: to inform readers about the subject or plot and give them a feel for how it is handled.

A synopsis is the author's primary selling tool and, together with the sample chapters, is the basis on which a publisher or agent will decide whether to consider the manuscript for publication.

Here are some general guidelines for writing your synopsis.

Style

Be factual and succinct. Use the present tense and strong verbs and nouns, minimising adjectives. Avoid gratuitous information or overly detailed descriptions.

Length

Unless a publisher or agent specifies the length of the synopsis, keep it under 200 words (and double spaced, if presenting hard copy).

Structure

Include a headline, a succinct summary of your content (using new paragraphs for each main component), details of any notable contributors, and a brief note as to the target audience.

Presentation

Display your name and the title of your manuscript at the document (or top right-hand corner of each page if presenting hard copy) to prevent confusion should the synopsis become separated from the accompanying material.

When to write it

You may choose to compose it while writing your manuscript or at the end. Some manuscripts stay true to the synopsis, most deviate from it slightly, and a few take on a life of their own with the final product bearing little resemblance to the original synopsis!

Find what works for you, but remember that writing a synopsis early helps you stay in control of your material and stay on track.

Synopses and blurbs

Check out blurbs of published books in your genre or category, as they are written by marketing teams experienced in enticing readers. Be aware, however, that the function of a blurb is different to that of a synopsis.

Like a blurb, a synopsis should hook its readers in early by telling them what to expect and keeping them interested; unlike a blurb, a synopsis should give a full explanation of the subject and not leave unresolved questions. The teasing quality common to many a blurb, particularly in fiction, is not appropriate to a synopsis. A blurb is pitched at readers to whet their appetite and make them want to buy a book; a synopsis is aimed at publishers or agents to inform them about a manuscript with the long-term aim of making them want to publish it.

Fiction synopses

Typically, a fiction synopsis should cover these areas:

- What genre does the book fall into? (e.g. thriller, romance, fantasy)
- What is the main plot and sub-plots? What are the main scenes?
- Who is/are the main protagonist/s, and what are their goals?
- What are the problems confronting the main protagonist/s, and what are the consequences if they are not solved?
- How or to what extent are the problems ultimately resolved, and at what cost to the protagonist/s? (i.e. resolution and conclusion)

Here is an example of a synopsis of an historical fiction book:

> *Historical fiction about the controversial Saint Jerome is given a contemporary twist*
>
> Rome, 382 AD. When the Pontiff commissions Jerome to translate the Bible into Latin, it is a political masterstroke. Jerome's Vulgate displaces the many alternative biblical texts and plays a critical role in establishing Christianity as a world religion. Yet Jerome is his own worst enemy and quickly alienates the ruling elite, many of whom are targets of his famously sarcastic wit.
>
> What is less known is that Jerome is assisted by a circle of aristocratic women who risk their lives in the pursuit of their ideals. Chief among them is the attractive young widow Paula,

as devoted to Jerome as she is to his cause. Rumours circulate as his enemies plot to dispose of Jerome once and for all …

Includes a Foreword by Richard Johnson, Emeritus Professor of Classics, Australian National University.

Will appeal to readers of historical fiction, especially those interested in Ancient Rome, Christianity, and the often surprising role of women in the ancient world.

Nonfiction synopses

Typically, a nonfiction synopsis should cover these areas:

- What genre does the manuscript fall into? (e.g. educational, journalism, self-help). Note that the sub-genre of 'creative nonfiction' includes literary journalism, memoirs, biographies, travel and food writing.
- Who is the intended audience?
- What is the central theme or argument, and how is it presented?
- How is the theme broken down and explored, what are the counter-arguments or alternative solutions, and how are they addressed?
- What is the conclusion?

Here is an example of a synopsis of a nonfiction book on drawing:

A step-by-step guide to drawing for anyone seriously interested in drawing

This book is aimed at anyone who wants to learn to draw, whether for pleasure or professionally. Clearly written and copiously illustrated, it consists of an introduction and 12 drawing projects.

The reader is introduced to various materials and equipment, including pencils, crayons, pastels, charcoal and chalk, and pen and ink.

The projects offer step-by-step textual explanations and corresponding drawings demonstrating the development from rough sketch to finished artwork. The reader learns to match materials with subjects and styles – for example, coloured pencils for a depiction of flowers or buildings, and charcoal for tonal contrast in draped material.

The reader's power of observation is sharpened as the principles behind identifying the light source are explained: applying light and dark shading, colour blending, and proportion and perspective.

By the end, readers will understand the basics of drawing and be able to create their own individual artworks.

Edited by A M Erhenberg, Director of School of the Art Institute of Chicago.

Will appeal to students of fine art as well as the interested amateur artist.

Selecting sample chapters

Sample chapters are provided by the author to a publisher, literary agent or other interested party to enable them to get a feel for the manuscript and how it is written.

Select your strongest chapters, and ones that are representative of the whole. Some publishers specify how many sample chapters they require (usually varies between one and three). If they don't, submit two or three. They don't necessarily have to be the first chapters; more important than the number of chapters selected is that they are varied and display to advantage the different facets of your writing.

To represent fiction, select a range of chapters. Avoid including the first or last chapter, as beginnings and endings are notoriously difficult to write and any weakness in the writing is often revealed; also avoid choosing chapters that are sequential as this can narrow the apparent scope of your writing. For the same reason, if you submit two chapters, it is often a good idea to choose one from the first half of your manuscript, and the other from the second half.

To represent nonfiction, include the chapters that you feel most comfortable with, that contain central themes or arguments and, if suitable, a typical table, chart, graph or illustration.

With both fiction and nonfiction, a handy tip is to choose those chapters that 'wrote themselves' or that were least fraught with problems—they tend to be the most fluidly written. What we find easy to write, others find easy to read.

Writing a covering letter

This is what you use to introduce your manuscript proposal to a publisher or literary agent. It is usually accompanied by a synopsis and sample chapters.

Before writing your covering letter, contact the company or agent whom you wish to address to establish that they accept unsolicited manuscripts (i.e. manuscripts which they have not commissioned), and to make sure that they accept the genre of your manuscript. A telephone call or email will ensure that you don't waste your time, as well as giving you the opportunity to find out the name of the person to address and any other submission requirements. In publishing houses, this is usually the commissioning, or acquisitions, editor. If you're submitting electronically, you're usually required to complete the submissions section of the relevant web page.

Whether you're writing a covering letter to an editor, literary agent or anyone else, remember that their time is limited. Make sure your letter is factual and concise, and your tone professional.

The biggest single error people make when writing covering letters is to feel that longer and more detailed is necessarily better. Here are some tips to avoid that:

- Confine yourself to key facts, succinctly expressed (one page maximum).
- Address an individual, using the whole name if you're unsure of gender (e.g. 'Dear Andrea Carlsson' rather than 'Dear editor').
- State the purpose of your letter: either to find out whether an editor would like to consider your manuscript for publication, or to seek from a literary agent an opinion on its literary worth and publishing potential.
- List the contents of your submission. In addition to the covering letter itself, this is generally a synopsis and two or three sample chapters.
- Outline the subject matter and scope of your manuscript (a few lines), its genre (one line) and its intended audience (one line).
- Give the total word count, rounded off.
- List any previously published work or writing awards and, if pertinent, describe (briefly) any personal background work or experience.
- Electronic submission is preferable, being quick, safe and inexpensive. If you're requested to submit hard copy, include a SASE (self-addressed, stamped envelope) for the editor or literary agent to use to send their response. If appropriate, explain that you don't need the synopsis and sample chapters back.
- Display your contact details (i.e. address, telephone and email) clearly.

Here is an example of a typical covering letter addressed, in this case, to the commissioning editor of a publishing company:

14.9.17

Dear Lisa Chang

Following our telephone conversation, I am pleased to submit my manuscript *The Journey of Patrick O'Shaughnessy* for consideration for your genealogy and family history list.

I enclose a synopsis and two sample chapters, as requested.

It is a dramatised account of my great great great-grandfather's voyage by ship in the mid-1860s from County Kerry in Ireland to Wairoa in New Zealand. Based on family correspondence as well as documents from government archives and church records, the book explores his reasons for leaving, the challenges and hardship of the voyage out, and the adjustments he was required to make upon arrival.

Facsimiles of early letters and documents, including the ship's log, are included. The manuscript has historical interest as well as personal appeal.

The total word count is 65,000.

My previous work includes two poems, 'Forbidden world' and 'After the storm', published in 2008 in the literary journal *Images*.

I enclose a SASE for your reply. There is no need to return the synopsis and sample chapters.

Yours sincerely

Jim O'Shaughnessy

Address: 7B Villiers St, Tiki Punga, Whangarei, New Zealand
Tel: 4976 438
Email: jmoshaughnessy@yahoo.co.nz

Note: Refer to the Appendix for a covering letter template that you can copy and tailor to your individual needs.

Self-publishing or independent publishing

'A successful self-publisher must fill three roles: Author, Publisher, and Entrepreneur—or APE.'

Guy Kawasaki, graphics-design spokesperson and author

Self-publishing or independent publishing is fast becoming an established practice and gaining widespread credibility and community respect. Here, the author takes on the role of the commercial publisher, including responsibility for editing and design, printing and binding, and marketing and distribution.

This is not to be confused with 'vanity publishing'—so-called because it is perceived as appealing to the vanity of the author—which makes its money from fees charged to authors to publish their books, often irrespective of their quality. Largely for this reason, it is not held in high esteem within the book trade, nor condoned by established publishing associations.

Independent publishing is not new; authors have tried to get their work in print since publishing began. To go back to the relatively recent example of George Orwell: he had been trying to raise money to self-publish *Animal Farm* when Secker and Warburg decided to take it on.

The development of print-on-demand publishing platforms (such as Lightning Source and CreateSpace), however, makes it easier, quicker and cheaper than ever before to produce both a printed book and an e-book. Books are printed as and when the customer orders them with no requirement to set a fixed print run. The advantages for the author are obvious, but you still need to know the rudiments of book production as well as marketing in order to publish successfully. This also applies to e-books (in particular, ensuring that your conversion is carried out professionally and that readers can easily navigate their way around).

The inherent risk of this form of publishing is that, precisely because it is so easy and cheap, many authors economise on the editing and design of their books, so the overall quality of self-published books, once high, has deteriorated. Lack of structure and paragraphing, spelling errors and poor design are, sadly, common features of many self-published books. You would not buy a shirt where the collar is becoming unstitched: why would you buy a book where 'Foreword' is misspelled or there are multiple typos in the first few pages?

Here are some basic steps to follow to make sure that your self-published book is well published.

Editing

Once your manuscript is final and complete, have it edited professionally. The editor's role is to ensure that your writing is clear, correct and suitable for your proposed readership.

There are two levels of editing: copy editing and structural editing.

- Copy editing addresses grammar, spelling and punctuation as well as clarity of expression and consistency of style.
- Structural editing involves rewriting and restructuring material, and making other substantive suggestions for improvement.

Your local society of editors will contain a register of available editors where you may be able to find one who specialises in your genre.

First, get a quote. Some editors base their quotes on the number of words, others work to a flat fee, but usually editors copy edit up to 1500 words per hour maximum (less if editing structurally). Provide them with a sample of your manuscript and let them know of any concerns you may have so they can quote effectively. Once you have found an editor and agreed a quote, a schedule can be set.

Allow a reasonable timeframe for editing. It is meticulous work and, because they are approached at the end of the production process, editors are often pressured with unreasonable deadlines. Most editors work in Word using Track Changes, enabling you to view, and accept (or not) each change. After editing, allow extra time for you to approve all changes and resolve any outstanding queries.

When editing is complete and you have approved all changes, your manuscript is ready to be styled.

Design

While your manuscript is being edited, you can organise both your cover design and internal design, ensuring both conform to whatever specifications your print-on-demand company use.

Get the very best cover you can afford—it is your book's calling card, the first thing the reader sees. Whether you commission a designer to create an individual cover or buy a pre-made cover, make sure that your title and the author's name stand out clearly, and that any illustration is relevant to your subject matter. Avoid the tendency of many new authors of having too many competing elements on their covers; instead, opt for a clean, uncluttered look.

For your text design, again you can either commission an internal design, or buy one of the many templates available and drop your text into it. This is by far the cheaper option, but make sure that the template you choose contains all the elements that you need designing (e.g. headings, captions, quotes). Otherwise, you can waste time adapting it to your needs later, or hiring a designer to do so. Most importantly, ensure your text is finalised *before* it is dropped into a template.

Publishing

To set up your title for printing, you should obtain:

- ISBN (an international standard book number) which identifies your book to the distribution systems. Note that you will need separate ones if you're releasing both a print and an e-book.
- Barcode (which enables a book to be scanned, so is necessary for retail).
- Cataloguing in publication (CIP) data or a cataloguing statement. This is used by national libraries to categorise upcoming books for libraries and library suppliers. Optional and free, it helps give your book exposure.

Once your files have been accepted for printing and you have approved a review copy (strongly recommended), you're ready to publish!

Marketing

Once your book is published (and beforehand), you need to market it. Authors, including traditionally published ones, are increasingly shouldering a greater responsibility for their own marketing.

Despite the time this takes (including time taken away from writing), doing your own marketing brings definite advantages. No one knows your book better than you do yourself; you are in a unique position to 'present' it to prospective readers, selecting the strategies with which you're most comfortable.

There are various marketing packages available at a cost, and while they can be helpful in recommending the strategies best suited to your title and alerting you to new approaches, you still have to apply most of those strategies yourself.

Note that most book sales happen online, so it is important to do all you can to raise your title's online visibility.

Here are the most commonly used strategies in book marketing:

Website

Create an author's website for yourself or for your book or series of books, ensuring that it is 'mobile responsive'; that is, designed to adapt to mobile phones as well as computer screens. It does not need to be overly complex, but clear, informative and approachable. Update it regularly with news about your book (e.g. cover, blurb, extracts, reviews) as well as sales links or 'to buy' buttons.

Landing page

Put together a 'landing page' for each book (usually, but not always, part of your author's website) with a URL to which viewers can be directed. This page should gather all the key information about your book: blurb and author bio, cover image, review highlights, publishing data (price, ISBNs, pagination) and retail links.

SEO

Do whatever you can to increase your search engine optimisation (SEO) so that your book appears in as many online searches as possible. Pay attention to the keywords in your website and landing page and anywhere else where you post your promotional and related material.

Press release

Create one and disseminate it as much as possible. It should include a high-resolution front cover image, a strong, succinct blurb and author bio, review highlights and links to any interviews or adverts.

Reviews

Elicit reviews, both industry reviews (subject experts and other established writers in the genre) and customer reviews (particularly on Amazon). The more reviews your book has, the more interest it generates which pushes its ranking up, in turn generating more visibility.

Social media

Cultivate a presence and build up connections on social media (e.g. LinkedIn, Facebook, Twitter, Instagram and Pinterest). Join appropriate groups, both literary and promotional, and engage with other like authors. Post regularly, being careful to follow the rules regarding posting promotional material, or material that may be viewed as such. Take the same interest in the work of others that you would like your book to receive; explore the pages of the authors whose pages you follow or 'like' and show a continued interest in their progress and posts. Avoid the superficiality associated with much of social media interaction—aim instead to deepen discussions and forge genuine relationships rather than simply accruing friends, followers or 'likes'.

Amazon and Goodreads

Join Amazon, the world's biggest online store, and Goodreads, the world's biggest book club. Create an Amazon Author Page and join the Goodreads Author Program, and consider advertising your book within both forums or organising carefully timed giveaways.

Local community

Contact your local libraries and community centres to create interest in your book. There may be a centre where you could organise a launch with cut-price advance copies, or offer a talk or discussion together with a book-signing. Meeting the author is for most readers a powerful incentive to buy their book!

Advertise

Depending on your budget, advertise online. To maximise your reach, work out the demographics of your audience (e.g. age, gender, language and interests) and filter your adverts according to people's profiles.

Book trailer

Create a book trailer (maximum 90 seconds) with carefully selected visuals, script and music. Post it on your website as well as distributing it on YouTube and social media. Used strategically, a trailer pushes up your book's visibility enabling it to reach many who would otherwise not find out about it.

Email list/blog

Build up an email list and/or blog of relevant, interested readers with whom to connect and keep updated as to the progress of your book or books and other related topics of mutual interest.

Appendix: Standard forms and letters

This contains templates of standard forms and letters that can be photocopied and tailored to suit individual needs.

Style sheet template

Title: ....

ABC	DEF
GHI	**JKL**
MNO	**PQR**
STUV	**WXYZ**

Headings:

Lists:

Quotations:

Tables:

Illustrations:

References:

Other:

Permissions request template

(*date and address of copyright owner*)

Dear (*name*)

I would like to request your permission to use
(*details of extract/illustration/table/chart/graph or other*)

from your publication:
(*title, author, publisher, year of publication, page. no.*).

A copy of this material, together with the appropriate manuscript page, is enclosed to show the context in which it would appear.

Details of my manuscript/forthcoming publication in which I would like to use it are:
(*title, author, publisher, projected date of publication*).

Full acknowledgment will appear as a footnote/credit line.

Should you have any query, please do not hesitate to give me a telephone call or email me.

I would be grateful if you would reply in writing by
(*date—allow three weeks*).

Yours sincerely

(*name*)

(*contact details: address, telephone, email*)

Artwork brief template

Title:.......................................

Artwork #	Ms page #	Size	Description	Notes/source

Covering letter template

(*date and address of editor/agent*)

Dear (*name of editor/agent*)

I would like to submit my manuscript (*manuscript title*) for consideration for your (*fiction/nonfiction*) list.

I enclose a synopsis and (*two/three*) sample chapters, as requested.

My manuscript is about (*brief outline/genre*). It is intended for (*specify readership*).

It has a total of (*word count*).

My previously published work includes (*list titles*).

I have the following credits or awards (*list titles*).

My background work or experience is (*give brief details, if relevant*).

I enclose a SASE for your reply. There is no need to return the synopsis and sample chapters.

Yours sincerely

(*name*)

(*contact details: address, telephone, email*)

Glossary: Common terms in printing and publishing

This covers some commonly used terms in writing, publishing and printing.

arabic numerals the 10 digits from 0 to 9 used, among other things, for numbering the main text of a book, so-called because they were introduced into Europe by Arab scholars and established there during the Middle Ages (also referred to as Hindu–Arabic numerals, because Hindus in India had invented the symbol for zero and a modern decimal place value system by the sixth century, thus making arithmetic calculation far easier than with the abacus).

bold a heavy, thickened weight of typeface, particularly suited to highlighting key words or phrases and make them visually compelling (as in this glossary).

cropping trimming the edges of a picture, usually a photograph, and reframing it to accentuate the most important aspect and improve its overall composition; can be done in photo editing software or on hard copy by masking the unwanted areas.

em rule (—) commonly called a 'dash', it measures approximately the width of a capital 'M', and is used primarily as a separating device to indicate an abrupt break in a sentence or to introduce an explanation.

en rule (–) based on the width of a lower-case 'n', this is most commonly used as a linking device in spans of numerals or time, or to indicate an association between equivalent words.

folio refers to a sheet of paper folded over to make two leaves (four pages) of a book or manuscript; also used more loosely to refer to the front sides of each leaf (from the Latin *folium*, meaning 'leaf').

font (or fount) a specific variant within a family of typefaces (e.g. bold, roman and italic are varieties of font within a typeface) because historically every new variant in font had to be cast individually; now that variations in type are achieved digitally, the terms 'font' and 'typeface' are, predictably, often confused (derived from Old French *fonte*, meaning 'founding' or 'casting').

format applied to text, this refers to how text is displayed (including the style of headings or captions, whether paragraphs are spaced or indented, and whether text is justified, flush left or centred); applied to a book, this refers to its size, shape and general physical appearance (specifically, how many times the original sheet has been folded to form the leaves) (from the Latin *liber formatus*, meaning 'volume formed').

halftone a tonal value midway between high light and dark shade, achieved by means of breaking up an image into a series of dots or pixels and simulating a continuous tone; the term refers to both the technique and to the picture created by it (in particular, black-and-white photos).

house style the set of stylistic conventions observed by a publishing company, covering matters such as variant spellings and capitalisation, and the presentation of body text including headings, captions and displays.

italic a slanting typeface used to emphasise the meaning of a word or short phrase (e.g. *italic* ***italic*** *italic*) (based on the cursive letterforms used by sixteenth-century Italian calligraphers, designed for speedier and more compact writing).

justified text refers to setting type so that all lines are of an equal length, achieved by adjusting the space between words, and sometimes between letters within words; 'unjustified' text is usually referred to as 'flush left' or 'ragged right' (from the Latin *justificare*, meaning 'to make just').

landscape refers to the orientation of a page or illustration that, being wider than it is tall, is placed sideways, or horizontally, with its left side at the base.

leading (pronounced 'ledding', also called line spacing) refers to the extra space inserted between lines of type, measured from baseline to baseline, and estimated in points (e.g. 12 pt Times set on 14 pt leading, or 12/14 pt) (derived from the strips of lead placed between lines in the days of hot metal type).

legibility refers to the speed with which each letter or word can be recognised or deciphered, and is concerned with typeface design (e.g. point size, line length, word and letter spacing, number of capitals, text alignment and background colour).

manuscript literally, a document written by hand, now widely used to refer to the author's original copy of a document that is handwritten or typed, as opposed to printed or otherwise reproduced (from the Latin *manu scriptus*, meaning 'written by hand').

number describes the concept of quantity and includes both numbers expressed in figures or symbols (i.e. numerals) as well as those spelled out as words (e.g. 7, VII and seven are all numbers).

numeral a number expressed in figures or symbols rather than words (e.g. 8 *or* VIII *rather than* eight) (from the Latin *numerus*, meaning 'number').

orphan the first line of a paragraph that falls on its own at the bottom of a page or column, separated from the remainder of the paragraph.

pagination the numbering of both sides of each page of a book or manuscript, as opposed to 'foliation', in which only the folios, or front sides of each leaf, are numbered (from the Latin *pagina*, meaning 'vine trellis', 'leaf' or 'column of writing').

point a traditional Anglo-Saxon unit of measurement equal to 0.35 mm, or one twelfth of a pica, still used to express type size and leading; 10–12 point is standard for continuous printed text, and 12 point the default setting for on-screen type, with leading usually two points larger (e.g. '10/12 pt Garamond' describes a 10 point Garamond type size set on 12 point leading).

portrait refers to the orientation of a page or illustration that, being taller than it is wide, is placed upright, or vertically.

readability refers to the ease with which a printed page is read, and is concerned with content and expression (e.g. Is the text interesting and well expressed?) as well as overall design and layout (e.g. Is the design inviting?)

recto the right-hand page of a book, which always has odd numbers (from the Latin *rectus*, meaning 'right' or 'upright').

roman a medium-weight upright typeface (as opposed to bold or italic), ideal for body text (e.g. **cat** cat cat) (designed in fifteenth-century Italy, based on the script used in ancient Roman inscriptions).

roman numerals the numeral system used by the ancient Romans, based on Etruscan tally marks, and still used for numbering the preliminary pages of books (lower case, e.g. i, ii, iii) or chapters, parts or sections (upper case, e.g. I, II, III) (the lack of a symbol for zero and the unwieldiness of large numbers disadvantaged the Roman counting system compared with the Hindu–Arabic numerals which eventually replaced it in the fourteenth century).

sans serif (or sanserif) refers to a design of typeface without the small lines, or serifs, at the extremities of the main strokes of letters, the clarity of which suits single lines or short blocks of text such as in signs, headings or children's books, as well as on-screen text (e.g. **h** rather than **h**).

serif refers to the small lines at the extremities of the main strokes of letters, making them highly legible and suitable for body text, although less so for on-screen text (e.g. **h** rather than **h**) (derived from the Dutch *schreef*, meaning 'stroke' or 'line'; the style is derived from imitating the brush marks around ancient Roman inscriptions).

typeface a 'family' of designed type with its own unique style, including an alphabet, numerals and punctuation marks (e.g. Arial, Garamond and Helvetica).

verso the left-hand page of a book, which always has even numbers (from the Latin *verso*, meaning 'to turn over').

widow the last line of a paragraph that falls at the top of the following page or column, separated from the remainder of the paragraph.

Bibliography: Dictionaries and recommended resources

These books span five categories: standard dictionaries used in various English-speaking countries; general writing and editing resources; established style manuals; texts whose quality of writing and universal appeal have rightly won them near-classic status; and modern texts that are light-heartedly instructive.

Language dictionaries

Canadian Oxford Dictionary 2004, 2nd edn, ed. K Barber, Oxford University Press, Don Mills, Ontario. (Canada)

Macquarie Dictionary 2017, 7th edn., The Macquarie Library Pty Ltd, Sydney. (Australia)

Oxford South African Concise Dictionary 2011, 2nd edn rev., Oxford University Press, Goodwood, South Africa. (South Africa)

The New Zealand Oxford Dictionary 2004, ed. T Deverson & G Kennedy, Oxford University Press, Australia. (New Zealand)

The Oxford English Dictionary 1989, 2nd edn, ed. J Simpson & E Weiner, Oxford University Press, Oxford. (UK)

Webster's Third New International Dictionary of the English Language Unabridged 1993, ed. PB Gove, Merriam-Webster Inc., Springfield, Massachusetts. (USA)

Writing and editing resources

Baldick, C 1991, *Concise Oxford Dictionary of Literary Terms*, Oxford University Press, Oxford.

Butcher, J 2006, 4th edn, *Copy-Editing: The Cambridge Handbook for Editors, Authors and Publishers*, Cambridge University Press, Cambridge.

Leland, CT 2002, *The Creative Writer's Style Guide: Rules and Advice for Writing Fiction and Creative Nonfiction*, Writer's Digest Books, Cincinnati, Ohio.

Manners, C 2004 (repr.), *Clear Writing: A Guide to Current Grammar and Usage*, Sydney, Cromarty Press.

Peters, P 2004, *The Cambridge Guide to English Usage*, Cambridge University Press, Port Melbourne.

Ritter, R 2005, *New Hart's Rules: The Handbook of Style for Writers and Editors*, Oxford University Press, Oxford.

Roget's Thesaurus of English Words and Phrases 2004, ed. G Davidson, Penguin, London.

The Concise Oxford Dictionary of English Etymology 1996, rev. edn, ed. TF Hoad, Oxford University Press, Oxford.

Tredinnick, M 2006, *The Little Red Writing Book*, NewSouth Publishing (UNSW), Sydney.

Style manuals

MLA Handbook 2016, 8th edn, Modern Language Association of America, New York.

Publication Manual of the American Psychological Association 2009, 6th edn rev., American Psychological Association, Washington DC.

Ritter, R 2016, 3rd edn rev., *New Oxford Style Manual*, Oxford University Press, Oxford.

Style Manual for Authors, Editors and Printers 2011, 6th edn, John Wiley & Sons, Australia

The Chicago Manual of Style 2017, 17th edn, University of Chicago Press, Chicago.

The Economist Style Guide 2015, 11th edn, Profile Books, London.

Classic texts

Fowler's Modern English Usage 2004, 3rd edn rev., ed. RW Burchfield, Oxford University Press, Oxford.

Gowers, Sir E 1987, *The Complete Plain Words*, 3rd edn, rev. S Greenbaum & J Whitcut, Penguin Books Ltd, London.

Murray-Smith, S 1990, 2nd edn, *Right Words: A Guide to English Usage in Australia*, Penguin, Ringwood Vic.

Orwell, G 1946, 'Politics and the English language' in *George Orwell: Essays* (intro. B Crick), Penguin Classics, London, 2000.

Strunk, W Jr & White, EB 2000, *The Elements of Style*, 4th edn, Allyn & Bacon/Longman Publishers, Needham Heights, Mass.

Modern texts

Bragg, M 2004, *The Adventure of English: The Biography of a Language*, Sceptre, London.

Eco, U 2006, *On Literature*, trans. Martin McLaughlin, Vintage Books, London.

Hitchings, H 2009, *The Secret Life of Words: How English became English*, John Murray, London.

Truss, L 2009, *Eats, Shoots & Leaves: The Zero Tolerance Approach to Punctuation*, Harper Collins, London.

Index

CPSIA information can be obtained
at www.ICGtesting.com
Printed in the USA
LVHW011238300119
605791LV00004B/569